Yon Green Garden

**The World of a
Little Girl
Remembered**

*To Jill
Best Wishes
Christine Chadwick.*

Christine Chadwick

Riviera Press

First published in the UK in 2012 by
Riviera Press in paperback
Copyright © Christine Chadwick

ISBN 978-1-908945-01-3

Cover and text design by Ruth V Pittam
Printed and bound in the UK

1st Floor, Imperial House
50 Torwood Street
Torquay
Devon TQ1 1DT

My sincere thanks go to:

Gail Tucker
Janet Butlin
Claire Chilcott

For their unstinting help and practical advice

And to Keith

for his support and encouragement.

PREFACE

There have been many childhood memoirs published in recent years. Many of them have been sad, childhoods blighted with poverty and hardship, illness and abuse, stories that were immensely moving and disturbing. 'Yon Green Garden' is not like that. I was a happy child, my childhood was sheltered, safe, secure, like a garden where the plants are nurtured and cherished, but beyond the garden gate, the weeds take over and the harsh stony ground is exposed.

My memories are of everyday life, the pattern of life in a world that has now disappeared, memories of family and people I knew, places I visited, things I was told and things I overheard.

Now Yorkshire has been left far behind. I moved to Devon almost forty years ago with my husband Keith, our two lovely sons, Philip and Stuart and my dad. My mother had sadly died some years earlier and Dad was alone and not in good health. It was a wrench in many ways, but the time seemed to have come for a move, but where should we go? Scarborough can be so cold when the East wind comes off the North Sea and York has no sea at all, while Paignton has a balmy climate and palm trees growing on the seafront!

Devon has been good to us. As members of the Salvation Army we spent much of our spare time in its activities – Keith and the boys in the band and I was involved with the Sunday school and Young People's activities for many years. Keith worked for a local engineering company and this eventually led to him starting his own business.

The world of 'Yon Green Garden' is far away. Or is it? Is it not a fact that the pattern of our childhood sets the foundation of our adult lives? I believe it does, and that my experiences so long ago have contributed to the person I am now.

I hope you will enjoy sharing in these memories, which I dedicate to my mother.

July 2011

CONTENTS

CHAPTER ONE

'I will take thee to yon green garden
Where the pratty flowers grow,
Where the pratty, pratty flowers grow.'
Holmfirth Anthem.

My childhood was spent in a world that has long-since disappeared; a world where a child had space and freedom. Of course, I lived in the country, in the old West Riding of Yorkshire, in Holmfirth, which has become famous in recent years as the setting for the TV series 'Last of the Summer Wine'. A child then had the freedom to dawdle on the way to school, to day-dream, to play endless games of make-believe and explore the fields and woods and lanes, and time to cultivate that most precious of God's gifts, imagination.

Childhood is a time of vivid emotions, experiences and images. Much of it becomes blurred with time and is absorbed into the subconscious to form the foundations of the life and personality of the adult, but many images remain with startling clarity. It could be the picture of the corner of a room that returns with striking force, the rest of the room, hazy. It could be the scent of clean sheets and pillow cases laid tidily in a drawer, the sound of a creaking floorboard, the taste of fresh brown bread and Cheshire cheese, the sound of a brass band in the distance, with the music wafting away on the wind. These are the flavours of my childhood.

Figure 1.1
Holme village and valley

I have been happily married now for more years than I care to count, with two lovely sons and a much loved grandson. The places so dear to me as a child have been left behind, but Yorkshire remains in my blood. I have a deep and lasting love for Holmfirth and the world I once knew. Most of my life since the birth of my boys has been spent in bringing them up and working with children of all ages, in school, in playgroup and in Sunday school. It has been a joy and a privilege, but the contrast between the life of a child now and my childhood some sixty odd years ago is great indeed.

A few details will help to establish the time and place. I was born in 1938 and lived with my parents in Huddersfield. My father, Harold Strange, was a Huddersfield man, son of a hairdresser   immortalised by his shop sign 'A Strange Hairdresser.' It was a long established business, employing at that time my father, Uncle Vic, Cousin Mary and Grandad Strange him-self.

My mother was a country girl from Holmfirth, Constance 'Connie' Wagstaff. She was the only child of the daughter of a 'Gentleman' (so designated on the marriage certificate!) and a very talented painter and decorator, possibly the poorest branch of a quite extensive family of Wagstaffs.

As a young child the only people I knew to have a telephone and a car were the Vicar and the Doctor. Radio and the newspapers were the principal means of communication, houses were heated by a coal fire, food was rationed, washing was done in a tub with posser and mangle, and the front door was regularly left unlocked while Mam was out shopping. A different world indeed!

Through all my childhood reminiscences the place I remember most clearly and with the greatest affection is Holmfirth, and in particular, Ivy Cottage, where my closest family was rooted. The cottage was home, with all that is implied of love and security.

I have loved flowers and plants all my life and the garden which Grandad created there was surely where it all started. It was there I first planted seeds with him, and pricked them out, carefully lifting each tiny plant from the soft compost into a larger box, using one of Grandma's three-pronged forks. It was there I learned to recognize plants and to identify them by name and season, where I discovered mint, chives with their individual scent and taste. I loved the rosettes of leaves of London Pride and its tiny pink flowers growing in clusters on the red stems, and where Mam and I joked about the Lily of the

Valley which never thrived and was 'more valley than lily'!

Figure 1.2
The garden at Ivy Cottage
in its heyday

I marvelled at the huge orange oriental poppies, how the petals burst from the buds like crushed tissue paper which smoothed out in the sunshine, and when you looked into the flower the centre was black, with black pollen! There was a double peony, and it seemed that each year the blooms would appear, flawless and dramatic, and within a few days the weather would change and the rain and the wind would spoil them, leaving the ground covered with crimson petals. I looked forward each year to the scent of the pinks,white pinks, which Grandad had planted under the garden seat, and to the tall white marguerites, rather cruelly referred to as dog daisies. When we moved to Ivy Cottage, I spent many happy hours rummaging through the old tins and jars in the greenhouse, examining the old tools and the packets of seeds, which I sometimes planted.

My friends Anita, Margaret and Olwynne and I organised funerals for the occasional dead bird, frog or bumble bee which met their end in the garden, and one year, sadly, the body of one of our little dog Wendy's pups. The garden was an ideal place for our games of make-believe.

It was in this lovely garden that I dreamed my way through child-hood, reading book after book, and later re-vising for my 'O' levels, smothering myself in olive oil, or the newly available Nivea Cream, in a vain attempt to acquire a sun tan as I studied. This is my 'Yon Green Gar-den'. In my memory it is an ideal place, a source of so much pleasure and delight. It is like my childhood, sepa-rate, self-contained, but its influence continuing into every aspect of my experience and my life. The flowers I first knew there have found their way into every garden I have had since.

*

The far West of the old West Riding of Yorkshire is a place of high moorland, bleak and windswept in summer and desolate and menacing in winter. Holme Moss, which now houses the television mast and transmitting station, is one of the highest stretches of moor and is crossed by a narrow road, winding up the hillside, 'over the tops' and down the other side into Lancashire. For centuries, this was an important trade route. The local weavers took their cloth and sold it in Greenfield, Rochdale, Oldham and Manchester. The sides of the road are marked by by posts bearing a red reflective disc, not just at three or four feet from the ground, but also at six or eight feet, so they remain visible when the snow is drifting up the hillside and the blizzards are raging.

Figure 1.1
The Holme Valley from Holme Moss

Standing on Holme Moss in summer time, you can hear in the wind the call of the curlew and the skylark's song. The round-bladed grasses and the white tufts of cotton grass are bleached by the sun and the wind and seem to lie almost horizontal to the ground. The rounded hills are divided by deep gullies where the peat soil is visible and outcrops of rock where you may disturb a sheep or two, sheltering from the constant wind: a tough, harsh landscape, enduring and strong, like the people who are raised there. From this high moor, the view down the valley of the River Holme is breathtakingly beautiful, and now when I visit, tears come to my eyes and a lump to my throat. The river, scarcely big enough to merit the name at this point, flows down the valley and a series of reservoirs have been created, lonely, beautiful, reflecting the sky in their still waters. And lower down still, the first farms and houses, and still, even today, old mills, with chimneys pointing to the sky, empty now of smoke.

About a mile to the South East a similar stream, the Ribble, tumbles its way down a little valley, and in the small town of Holmfirth, the rivers meet. It was in this little valley that I lived from the age of about seven, in the cottage owned by my grandparents, bought soon after their marriage at the turn of the century, and where my mother had been born.

The rivers were the life blood of the valley, soft flowing water from the hills above, soft enough to wash the wool and then the cloth, sufficient supply to use for dyeing and, I suppose at one time for power. The mills had grown astride the rivers, taking the work out of people's homes where the cloth had been hand woven for centuries, and the whole process became industrialised. That was a stormy and violent time, when Luddites met in secret on the moors and planned attacks on the mills in a vain attempt to preserve their craftsmanship, their work and their slender income. Houses can still be seen with rows of windows in the upper storey, some now blanked off, revealing their origins as weaver's cottages. The upstairs was known as the loom chamber, upstairs for the best light.

Mills in the West Riding were often given splendid names: Perseverance Mill, Providence Mill, as well as being named after the place, Washpit Mill, Dover Mill and so on. My walks as a child took me from Ivy Cottage along Dover Lane to Dover Mill, passed the mill dam and further up the stream to Washpit Mill, a much bigger concern. Washpit Mill employed many men and women in those days, weaving, I suppose, cloth for military uniforms, and later, fine worsted cloth for export. I remember my mother hearing with some consternation that there were many Estonians working there, with scarcely a smattering of English. 'Fancy, here in Holmfirth! Whoever would have believed it?' They were displaced persons from Eastern Europe, I suppose, victims of the War. Washpit Mill yard, which had to be crossed as the shortest way to the dam and the pleasant walks beyond, was an exciting place to me. You may, if you were lucky, hear some of the Estonians talking to each other, and wonder what they were saying and whether it was really safe to be there!

There was noise, clatter of looms and hum of machines, men's voices, a woman laughing; the smells were strong, of ammonia and raw greasy wool, stinging the nostrils and hurrying you along. In the heart of the mill was the mill engine, beating its regular rhythm and humming smooth gleaming with polished brass and smelling of warm engine oil. It was named Agnes, after a well-loved member of the family who founded the mill.

Beyond the mill, you were out into the open again, where it was quiet at last which was the best miracle of all, where the river ran clear and lovely. The golden kingcups flowered under the trees at the far end of the old dam; frogspawn and newts were there in the spring, and pussy willow, and hazel catkins.

Washpit was the first mill to straddle the river. Downstream of it, the water was stained with dye and swarf, some days, dark grey or blue, according to what colours the dye house was using. The pollution was vile, for even on Sundays when the mills were closed and the water ran clear, the stones were coated with grey swarf, and fronds of the stuff floated like seaweed in the clear water. It was well worth the long walk to leave all that behind and find the true, lovely countryside, and follow the clear stream up on to the moor.

Figure 1.3
Cottages in
Underbank

Holmfirth itself can hardly be described as a pretty town. The two small rivers meet in the town centre, and in fact, part of the main street is a bridge. Several hundred yards upstream is another bridge, Upperbridge, over the River Holme. The hills rise quite steeply on either side of the river, with the old stone cottages seemingly stacked upon each other. The roads, little wider than lanes, provide access to the houses. They wind steeply up the hillsides, often surfaced with 'setts' or cobbles. Frequently linking one row of houses to the next above it, were shallow, and not so shallow, steps.

All the buildings are of the local stone; the millstone grit so abundant on the Pennine moors. It has a lovely mellow hue when clean, but a century of smoke from the mill chimneys has darkened the whole aspect, and with the steepness of the hills, there is almost a sense of brooding about the town, even today. No, I would never have described it as pretty. I think that would have been quite uncharacteristic of the people of Holmfirth, who no doubt would consider that description to be rather frivolous. It is practical, enduring, and has a defiant strength which will-will not be destroyed by flood or tempest, and indeed has been tried by both, for weather conditions here in the Pennines can be harsh, plenty of rain, plenty of snow, winds straight from the Moss to cut you in two, and a history of three terrible floods, when reservoirs on the moors above the town burst their banks and devastated the Valley.

Beauty there is in full measure in the surrounding hills, and somehow, it is this combination of strength and defiance, endurance and beauty that gives the area its undoubted charm. Although the town centre is small, it is, it is surrounded by many clustering villages and is a big meeting place.

In my childhood, as now, there were many public houses. Serious drinking places where women did not go! There were two banks and two churches; the Parish Church which we used to attend, and the Wesleyan Chapel (even after it became Methodist, it was always referred to as the Wesleyan Chapel) where Grandma used to attend something known as the 'Bright Hour' because, she said, it was more friendly than the Mothers Union!

Figure 1.4
The view of Underbank from the top road

The cemetery was up on a hill, away from the Parish church, but around the Chapel were many graves and I used to be quite worried by the fact that they had the appearance of stone boxes - upright slabs of stone with slabs of stone laid over the top, with an inscription.

Figure 1.5
Holmfirth Parish Church

Shops were all individually owned, except for the Co-op (pronounced, 'CWOP') where you had to give your membership number each time you bought anything, then you were given a check - receipt- which you had to stick on to a long sheet of paper at home. At the end of the year (or maybe half year) this was handed in and a dividend would be paid to you, according to how much you had spent. Grandma did this religiously and I would be sent to the Co-op whispering her number, 692, so as not to forget it. I never have! Of course, rationing was an ever present problem during the war, and each family had to register with one butcher and one grocer for their weekly necessities.

If the town had its own distinctive character, the same could certainly be said of the people who lived there; hard-working, fiercely individualistic, hospitable people, who chose their words well, and whose humour was so dry, not heavy handed, but finding its target with deadly accuracy. Thrift was a highly prized virtue and very occasionally, ran over into meanness. In fact, it was said of one woman who kept a shop in Underbank, that she would cut a currant in two! She was, according to Mam, a 'nipscrat'. Such an attitude was not at all typical however, and people seemed always ready to open their homes and entertain friends and family to huge high teas with cakes and trifle, pork pies and cold meats and pickles, or bread and jam if that was all the larder could yield. Home- made food was always preferred and baking and home making skills in a woman were regarded as essential.

The men were most likely to be employed in the mill as were many women. Traditionally, there were many jobs in the textile industry which were suited to women, spinning, mending, burling etc, and in fact, my mother worked as a mender for many years. When she left school at twelve years of age, she started her working life apprenticed to a tailor, but I imagine that the aftermath of the Great War prevented her from completing it, and into the mill she had to go.

They were an undemonstrative breed of people, who despised anything considered 'soft', and took a kind of grim pride in the steepness of the hills, the hardships of life, and the ferocity of the weather!

Nevertheless, they had their softer moments. Ac

cording to my Dad, whimsical tales abounded in the pubs, and music flourished. In fact, the valley and its environs boasted several brass bands which competed for, and won, many trophies in the contests of the North of England. Choirs there were in plenty, every village chapel, it seemed, managed to present 'Messiah' at Christmas, and 'Olivet to Calvary' at Easter. Many chapels also presented a pantomime, and there was a thriving Dramatic Society which had earned a fine reputation throughout the North. A Band Contest was held each year, and also a competitive Musical Festival.

Figure 1.6
Holmfirth without all the cars!

Hospitality and kindliness abounded, going hand in hand with what can only be described as nosiness. In an age when communication was limited, the war and national events seemed remote, and a journey even to the neighbouring towns and villages had to be on a bus or on foot. People were a close community, very interested in the comings and goings of their neighbours. Everyone knew everyone else, or so it seemed, and knew their father, and his father before him!

CHAPTER TWO

Family - the Strange side

The notion of a family to me remained one of idea rather than actuality. I was an only child of parents who were in their thirties at the time of my arrival. My mother was an only child too. My father was the youngest of four and we seldom saw my uncles and aunts, and my cousins were much older than me. There was no easy intimacy of brothers and sisters, no casual familiarity of cousins and aunts and uncles popping into Ivy Cottage, no opportunity for me to call in to see such relations on the way to and from school.

My mother's friends became my aunts: Auntie Jackman who lived next door before we moved to Ivy Cottage; Auntie Elsie and Uncle George in Holmfirth; Auntie Jessie and Uncle Ernest in Honley; and Alice in Jackson Bridge. The experience of teasing, of speaking your mind and knowing just how far to go, of seeking to get your own way in the face of sibling rivalry, was largely missing. I have rarely been without a friend and always preferred to have one or two close friends rather than be a member of a large group.

Looking back on my life I have usually faced new situations alone, first job, exams, new jobs, training events, even marriage and bringing up my children alone with Keith, my husband, but no other support!

My ideas of family however, were strong and re-

-main so. I had a firm belief in the family that I heard about from Mam, and I had a strong sense of my roots. She told me stories of her aunts and cousins and my Dad's brother and sisters, and I felt I belonged.

Grandad Strange I remember quite clearly, although we visited only once a year, on Boxing Day. He was an old man, inclined to stoutness, and had a shock of white wavy hair. Grandma Strange had been killed in a road accident before I was

Figure 2.1
Grandad Strange

born. I would like to have met her and often as a child I wondered what she was like. Word had it, in adult conversations which I innocently overheard, that she and Grandad had eloped together, although as I have never seen the marriage certificate or openly asked about it, I cannot vouch for the truth of that. I rather hope they did, it fits in with my idea of Grandad Strange as a wayward and determined character and adds a little softness and romance to the picture. However, I also heard dark comments of how he used to go to Scarborough for the weekend, leaving Grandma behind, and the heavy implication was that he went to meet a lady. He was a handsome man, arrogant and despotic as many an Edwardian man before him.

As a young man in Huddersfield he was apprenticed to a hairdresser, but in his early twenties his thick dark hair turned white. The proprietor took him to one side and said that, frankly, a young man with white hair was a poor advertisement for his business and he must either dye it, or leave. Young Alfred decided to dye it, and did so for many years. Eventually, he had a shop of his own, employing his two sons and his grand-daughter Mary, and when premises in Northumberland Street were acquired, the lettering on the wall was deliberately left without punctuation and read A STRANGE HAIRDRESS-ER. It was good publicity, a talking point, and added to his formidable reputation as the best hairdresser in Huddersfield.

In its heyday, the shop, the family business, must have been an impressive establishment, supporting during one period, three households and enjoying a fine reputation. People travelled many miles for Grandad to look at and treat various scalp problems, and were even recommended to him by the Huddersfield Royal Infirmary! There was a Waiting Room, a Ladies Room, and a Gentlemen's Saloon which had two hairdressing chairs, and washbasins linked by a stretch of beautifully curved white marble. Above that was a small glass shelf displaying hair creams, shaving brushes and soap, razors and shampoo. In those days, customers who needed measuring and fitting for a wig were seen confidentially. Hair was dyed, shampooed, cut, treated for scurf, split ends (by singeing with a lighted taper!) Alopecia or approaching baldness, but never curled or waved, styled or permed! Gentlemen went for a shave, with an open razor and the place was a hive of activity. Grandad was always to be seen in the fashionable hotels, especially the George, and the Conservative Club. Times were good and the business prospered.

His arrogance, however, led to his business demise. In the twenties when bobbed and shingled hair became the fashion among the young ladies, Grandad refused to cut off the long locks! He declared firmly that her hair was a woman's crowning glory and he would have no part in the short hair styles of the fashionable set. Inevitably, the customers went elsewhere, and in spite of the undoubted skill he had with the scissors; in spite of the lotions to cure alopecia and scurf and to stimulate the growth of hair on a balding pate; in spite of the confidential measuring for wigs (or transformations as they were sometimes known) and the diligent treatment of split ends with the lighted taper, the business gradually declined.

My Dad, who was too young for the First World War, being only twelve, was almost too old for the Second World War, but not quite, and in 1942 he was called up. In 1945, when peace was restored and the world was a different place, there was little room for businesses whose ideas were formed pre 1914!

In my memory, the shop was a dingy unattractive place. It was a semi-basement, beneath the Crescent Hotel and had an air of dereliction about it. The furniture was old and I can see now in my mind's eye the once elegant armchairs in the Waiting Room and the Ladies Room looking faded and tired, the stuffing just beginning to break through the well-worn leather covers. The mirrors looked dingy, not dirty, but the silvering had seen better days. The lino was worn, and the brush-grained panelling had not even had an extra coat of varnish since the place

29

had been first opened.

There was, I remember, a huge mirror in the Gentlemen's Saloon, such as you might find in a dance studio. I thought it magical, like a whole separate room, and I could dance and pose and pull faces in it. Of course I was vain, even then! The razor strops still hung conveniently to hand, but very rarely did anyone come for a shave. Dad and his elder brother Victor, my Uncle Vic, ran the shop at that time, Mary being needed at home as Grandad was by then quite elderly, and was a demanding character at best.

There was a small cubby hole of a place where Dad would boil his kettle and make up the lotions and potions. I was quite nervous of going in there; it was scary, with just the gas ring glowing underneath the old boiler, and the keen scent of the chemicals. Even scarier was the store room, which was actually under the pavement. This also housed the lavatory, so sometimes there was no escape - I had to go there! I remember sitting there, listening to the footsteps of passers-by over my head, and sometimes, someone would come down the steps to the shop, and I was so scared that instead of turning left into the shop, they would take a couple of extra steps and turn right and find me, and then what would I do? Of course, no one ever did.

Grandad's reputation, however, remained for many years. People would tell me of how they always had Mr Strange to cut their hair or their children's hair; of how his ointments had been so good and effective, and what an eccentric character he had been, but many customers went elsewhere and neither Dad nor Uncle Vic had sufficient money or initiative to build the business up again, and of course it is more than likely that Grandad kept his hand on it until his death, constantly refusing to modernise.

They had a cat at the shop at one time, which was fed on 'lights' from the butcher, lights being the lungs of a beast. Interesting things, you put them in a pan to cook them and they swelled up and if the pan was too small ....disaster! Cats loved them, in spite of the unappetizing smell. The shop cat knew exactly which pair of scissors was used to cut up his dinner! When anyone picked up 'his' scissors, he was there, at their feet, ready and waiting, in the manner of all knowing cats.

The tale was often told of Grandad and the sausages. He had bought the sausages from the local butcher, intending to fry them for his lunch. For some reason best known only to himself, he decided to wash them and filled the basin with water. A cry of shock and alarm went up. 'They float! The b--- sausages float! They must have lights in 'em! I'll not go to that butcher again!' Into the bin they went, or maybe they went into the cat?

Some customers, of course, had to be humoured and flattered. I reckon this was very hard for both Dad and Grandad, never gifted with a silken tongue at the best of times. I remember him talking of one lady who was a regular client, and wealthy with it, and in the course of conversation, he had remarked that a certain mutual acquaintance must be 'getting on a bit now'. She fixed him with a steely gaze and enquired 'And what does 'getting on a bit' mean, Mr Strange?' I don't know how he wriggled out of that one, but he almost lost a good customer.

Dad was particularly good with children, and one lady brought in her small boy, in something of a state, and said how difficult the child was at the barber's, and she was desperate to get his hair cut, but no one could do it! So Dad sat him in the chair, raised it up with the lever, chatted to him, took up his scissors and as he was about to start, the lady intervened with,

'Don't you want me to hold his ears?' Dad was astonished.

'Whatever for?' he asked.

'Well,' she replied, 'so that his head is kept still, that's what the other barber does,' to which Dad replied,

'Then it's no wonder the child cries! We'll have no nonsense of that kind in here.' Of course, the hair cut was completed with a minimum of fuss and no pain at all!

Dad always cut my hair, and Mam's and Grandma's too. I always had to wear it short with a side parting and a ribbon and, oh, I did want to grow it long and have plaits like my friends, but the threat of 'dicks' was always held out to me.

'Don't put on anyone else's cap, or hat, or beret. Don't put your head near anyone else's'. The warnings were dire, and delivered regularly. The horror stories of head lice were legion. In fact I heard so much about 'dicks' and nits that I found the prospect quite exciting and attractive, and when the day came and they were discovered in my head and something had to be done, I was quite pleased! The pleasure was short lived however, as Dad had to apply some very strong-smelling stuff which stung, and the whole process took ages and was very unpleasant indeed. When I passed the exam and went to the Grammar School, I was allowed to grow my hair as a reward, and I did actually achieve a length to have 'bunches', but I never managed to get it long enough for plaits. Then everyone else cut off their plaits so there seemed to be no point any more. I still couldn't have it waved of course, and in fact I must have been about twenty before I actually had another hairdresser to cut it.

I would curl it, with metal curling pins, but that was all, and I mustn't wash it more often than once a fortnight, as it would destroy all the natural oils! We had no hair dryer at home, so I would sit on the hearth rug, in front of the fire, to dry it. At one point, when I started working, I wanted a fringe and Dad refused to cut it for me, so I cut it myself, and not enough of it to lie forward (I have thick strong hair) so it had to be stuck in place each night with sticky tape! Dad was furious. I wasn't too happy either!

My visits to the shop, as a child, were infrequent, but it was there I met Uncle Vic, Dad's elder brother. He was a tall, thin man with a large nose and a slight stoop. I never knew him well. Auntie Elsie, his wife, I knew even less well. She was very small, with glasses and a nervous laugh. Their daughter Sylvia, my cousin, was a tall, sophisticated, confident young lady, good looking and stylish. It never ceased to amaze me that these three oddly assorted people had anything in common! They lived in a small terraced house down near the railway arches, on the edge of the Monday Market ground. I vaguely remember going to the house at Sylvia's wedding, to see the cake. Mam was very impressed with the fragility of the icing, it was truly lovely. Sylvia worked as a telephonist at the G.P.O. She was always very friendly when we met, but we never had any closeness, the age difference, I suppose, and the fact that we lived out at Holmfirth.

Our annual visits to Grandad Strange took place on Boxing Day and it was then that I would see Auntie Mabel and her daughter Mary. She too had a nervous laugh, she was the eldest daughter and she kept house for Grandad. It seems she was 'walking out' with a young man who was a soldier in the Great War. Having anticipated marriage, she found she was pregnant, but he was tragically killed in France before they could marry. In due course, Mary was born. Grandad did not turn her out, as many parents did in those days, but she suffered humiliation ever afterwards. Mary suffered the undoubted stigma of being illegitimate. Mabel had brought shame and disgrace on the family and, so far as I can see, was never allowed to forget it. She never married, nor did Mary. My mother never had much regard for Auntie Mabel's standard of cleaning having idly tapped the chair arm with her knitting needle and seen the dust rise, but then, as she said, when she is treated like an unpaid servant, can you blame her? Grandad would sit in the front room in his easy chair, his tall wooden ashtray-cum-what-not beside him, with ash scattered down his navy waistcoat. When the fire needed mending, he would call out 'Mabel! Coal!' and poor Auntie Mabel would come scurrying from the kitchen to put coal on the fire for him. No wonder she had a nervous laugh! She was a gentle, kindly soul, who worked hard to cook the large meals required by her father; he always kept a good table. She would cook goose on Christmas Day for Uncle Vic and his family and Auntie Phyllis and hers, and then a turkey on Boxing Day for our visit. When the meal was cleared away, we would all go into the front room and play cards - Newmarket or Twist, for half-pennies and pennies, and when I was considered old enough to join in some-times, I thought it great fun, but I never really felt at home there, never really at ease. I suppose, quite simply, we did not go often enough. The long journey from Holmfirth by bus and trolleybus was a problem.

Auntie Phyllis, Dad's youngest sister, was a favourite of mine, and perhaps even more than her, I was fond of Uncle Frank. They were closer in age to Mam and Dad, we used to visit them and they used to visit us, usually on a Sunday for tea. Uncle Frank was a dear, but like the rest of the clan enjoyed a drink more than was good for him. It was always a problem with the men, getting them home from the pub in reasonable time for a Sunday dinner, and to be able to catch the bus in time to visit for tea! Uncle Frank, I'm afraid, was known for rolling home, very merry, and emptying his pockets of money to give to any child he met!

Auntie Phyllis, in common with Dad and Grandad, could be rather brusque in her manner and dogmatic in her attitude, but underneath that tough façade, she was very tender, easily hurt. She was always very kind to me and I still have books that she gave me for birthdays and Christmas. She had formed the idea that my Mam loved Terry's Burnt Almonds (roasted almonds in very dark chocolate) and produced this treat every Christmas for her. Unfortunately, she was quite mistaken. Mam found them far too bitter, but never had the heart to tell her! So the gifts continued. She and Uncle Frank always had a dog, the bitches always being Sally and the dogs, Billy. One particularly exuberant Billy, a wire-haired terrier, leapt up at me in over friendly fashion and almost put me off dogs for life.

They had three children. The eldest, Kenneth, was brought up by Uncle Frank's sister, Mabel Lunn, for some reason I couldn't quite fathom. Apparently, Mabel took a great fancy to the little boy who was rather delicate, and as Auntie Phyllis was pregnant again quite quickly, Kenneth went to Mabel and stayed there. I always had the feeling that Auntie Phyllis felt she had lost her son. Barbara came along next. She went into the W.R.N.S. during the war and met a frightfully affluent chap and married him. He had 'no time for Northerners' and had no intention of marrying in Huddersfield. They had a registry office wedding in London, and I believe Barbara wore orchids on a very smart suit. They sent photographs, but I have the distinct impression that Auntie Phyllis and Uncle Frank were not invited. I could, of course, be quite wrong. Auntie Phyllis could be quite stubborn enough to have refused the invitation! Travel in wartime was difficult. At all events, she was hurt yet again; another child lost, no white wedding and no gathering of clans to celebrate; just a photograph, and tales of the inordinately expensive spray of orchids.

Molly, her youngest child, had a lovely white wedding, at Lockwood Church. She married Gordon, a local boy who was a pilot in the RAF, and from a very good family. Mam was very put out when I was not asked to be a bridesmaid. The phrases bandied about at home were 'not good enough, I suppose', and 'well, she isn't a pretty child, of course'. I have carried that remark with me ever since, it didn't do a lot for my confidence or self-esteem! Molly moved away after the wedding as Gordon continued in the RAF, so Auntie Phyllis and Uncle Frank were left alone, but their visits to Ivy Cottage continued and our visits to their home in Woodhead Road. When I was courting Keith, Uncle Frank had a very serious heart attack and was given only fifteen minutes to live. He survived, however, for many years. He never worked again, or drank again, but pottered happily in his garden and in the new greenhouse which his work colleagues at ICI had given him. After his death, Auntie Phyllis became a rather sad figure, even going out to work to clean the offices at the local brewery for a while, where she fed the office cat. She developed gangrene in her toe and had first one leg and then the other amputated. She stubbornly refused to move to Kent to live with Molly or with Barbara; Kenneth visited her every day, but she died at the age of eighty-nine, lonely and alone, but a fiercely independent fighter to the end. She was a dear, I loved her, and the image of her cottage stays fresh in my mind; the window was always full of flowers and flowering plants; there was always a welcome there, always a cup of tea, always served in china, with lump sugar.

These were Dad's family, the Stranges, and they were not close to me, except for Auntie Phyllis. Most of them I saw only at rare intervals, and they did not feature too much in Mam's conversations with me. Except, that is, when I displayed some behaviour of which she disapproved! Any signs of temper, arrogance or selfishness brought from her the comment 'that's the Strange coming out' or 'you are a Strange!' It was evident to me from a very early age that things between Mam and Dad were not too happy, hence all the bad things in my nature were attributed to him.

Dad saw his family, of course, at the shop, and when taking the week's money to Grandad's home in Marsh, in Huddersfield, on a Saturday evening. I have the distinct impression that they thought themselves just the smallest bit superior to my Mam. After all, they were town dwellers, Grandad was a well- known business man; they considered themselves to be sophisticated, while the Wagstaffs were country folk, their speech was broader, their horizons different, parochial, perhaps, but undeniably well-connected!

CHAPTER THREE

The Wagstaff Side of the Family Tree

The marriage certificate of Fred Wagstaff and Edith Shore, on the 26th of April 1903, states that Fred was a painter and decorator, son of John Wagstaff, labourer. Edith was the daughter of John Shore, Gentleman. My mother was often heard to remark that we were the poorest branch of the family, whether Shores or Wagstaffs, I couldn't say, but I imagine the marriage caused some consternation. Edith had married beneath her and Fred had done rather well! However, there was no animosity that I ever heard of; I expect Fred's undoubted charm won them over. Certainly there was some money around.

Figure 3.1 The Wagstaff Family, circa 1880. The children in the front row are, from left to right: Uncle Daniel, Auntie Beatrice, Uncle Beaumont, Auntie Phoebe and Fred, my grandfather

They bought Ivy Cottage, on Kippax Row in Underbank, and the land beside it which housed six derelict cottages, and as the years went by they transformed both the cottage and the garden. There were stories and photographs of visits to Cliftonville, Margate, Torquay, almost the equivalent of Florida in today's terms.

Grandma Wagstaff was an erect, dignified lady. Photographs show her to be quite plump, but I remember her as thin, energetic and very determined, Grandad was handsome, talented, and also very determined.

Figure 3.2
Grandad Wagstaff, on the right, looking very
UN-workmanlike

My mother was born in 1905, and during her childhood, the derelict cottages were places to play at 'house', hanging curtains at the gaping windows, making 'coffee' from the seeds of plantains, hanging out washed doll's clothes, but gradually, Grandad converted the space into a beautiful garden, with one of the original flights of stone steps leading up to the top garden. He it was who planted the cherry, the laburnum, the glorious double white lilac, who built a pond, and a rockery with a waterfall, the pump being housed in a little enclosed bunker which also housed his small clay flower pots. He grew most of their vegetables, covered the walls with ivy and climbing roses: Dorothy Perkins, Excelsior, and one which was a lovely creamy yellow in bud and became ivory white when fully open, the scent of summer.

He had a lean-to greenhouse, with a boiler house next to it to heat it in the winter months. And at the opposite end, the rain-water drained from the gutters into a large water tank.

He grew lovely ferns, tomatoes and chrysanthemums and won many prizes for his produce in the local shows. He would have rows of chrysanthemum cuttings in pots and bring them on outside through the summer while the tomatoes were in the greenhouse. Then, out would go the tomatoes and the pots

Figure 3.3
Grandma and Grandad Wagstaff
on their honeymoon.

of chrysanthemums, so lovingly disbudded and watered would be taken in.

The blooms were stupendous, tight, firm incurves, and shaggy Japanese varieties, big as mop heads. The scent was pungent, autumnal and heady. I can smell it now!

The greenhouse was a decided bonus, and the story of its building shows something of Grandad's individualism. He was very definitely a 'character', even, one might say a 'lovable rogue'!

It seems that the far end of his beautiful garden was the side wall of the neighbouring house. This was all well and good, but in the middle of this wall was a window, with a view right up Grandad's garden, destroying all privacy. Such a shame that the neighbours could see everything, watch when he was working, watch when he and Grandma had tea outside on the lawn, watch little Connie playing with her friends, and watch when the Wagstaffs had visitors who had to be shown the plants and the waterfall. Watch they certainly did, for nothing in Underbank escapes attention, and what can't quite be seen can be supposed! The problem of privacy was discussed at length and eventually the solution became clear. He waited until the neighbours were away on holiday and then, with the help of one or two friends, he built a wall of tongued and grooved planks six inches away from the neighbour's house wall, and built the greenhouse as a lean-to structure. The window was no longer a problem! What the neighbours said when they arrived home to find their window looked out on to darkness, I cannot imagine. There must have been a real rumpus, but the greenhouse stayed and the offending window remained in the room with closed curtains! In fairness, I must point out that the room in question also had a bay window which faced on to Kippax Row, so the room was not left entirely in the dark! I often wondered why those particular neighbours never spoke to us when everyone else was very friendly. When I was eventually told the full story I understood. I can't imagine that anyone could get away with doing such a thing nowadays, but Grandad managed it!

Grandma Wagstaff was a lady to her fingertips and had firm ideas about the décor of her new house. Where now we would seek to retain the character of an old cottage, then the idea was to present it as a rather grand residence, and the furniture, the curtains, blinds, and wallpaper and paint were fit for a mansion. Grandad had the skill in his fingers, and an eye for colour and style and a very lovely home was created. The doors upstairs he 'glazed', stippled or painted in some way to be a subtle shade of pink at the lower edge of each panel, gradually shading to cream at the top. The doors downstairs were 'grained', that is, painted to look like wood grain, with swirls and knots; varnished, and shaded to look like the most beautiful woods available. Their bed-

Figure 3.4
Grandma Wagstaff
with Connie,
my mother, as a baby

room furniture was of the most glorious red mahogany, with a polish that needed no elbow grease, just a leather, wrung out in vinegar and water, to keep it in tip top condition. They had a washstand and a dressing table, obtained from a wealthy mill owner whose house Grandad had doubtless decorated. Downstairs, a grey three piece suite, a mahogany sideboard, and a marble fireplace. When marble went out of fashion, Grandad painted and grained it to look like wood! They had a piano which Grandma played beautifully until rheumatoid arthritis crippled her hands. She knew what the houses of the gentry looked like, as indeed did Grandad in the course of his work, and everything at Ivy Cottage was done to emulate them.

They had lovely ornaments and pictures and several small plaster statuettes around the place, and when lifelike coloured statuettes went out of vogue, she persuaded Grandad to paint them all white, to look like marble. One in particular survives, a boy, known as Billy, watching a frog. Grandma finally prevailed on him to paint it white, but when he got to the frog, he couldn't bring himself to paint over the green, so, green it remained, and remains so to this day! He actually broke one of Grandma's statuettes, Venus, I think, and he fixed the head in the ivy covered wall over the garden seat, a constant reminder to be more careful next time.

Grandma was indeed a proud lady, and obstinate to a degree, and I imagine there were many battles of will between them. My memories are of her as an old lady, after Grandad's death in 1945. She was far from well, and eventually Mam, Dad and I went to live with her. She kept her own eccentric ways and she insisted on making what she called butter but which was merely the top of the milk left on a saucer and added to each day. She would put this on her bread and the smell must have been awful! From time to time she decided to bake some bread, and as she couldn't get along with Mam's new electric cooker, she found her own ancient gas cooker. It was much like a large biscuit tin, and she set it up in the wash kitchen and ran a length of rubber pipe to the gas tap near the washbasin in the bathroom (wash kitchen and bathroom were adjacent, upstairs) It was a lethal contraption and filled Mam with dismay, but Grandma's determination overruled her misgivings. She went to the local shop and bought flour and yeast, which she called, ' barm', and kneaded it as well as her poor arthritic hands would allow. I don't think the craze lasted long, to everyone's relief!

Soon after that, she suffered a stroke and was bedridden, paralysed down one side. Mam nursed her, toileted her, washed the sheets every day, looked after me, endured Dad's disapproval of living in Holmfirth, and attempted to keep the garden in order. As Grandma recovered, through sheer willpower, Mam was able to relax a little, but not for long. Grandma was as determined as ever to do her own thing, and as soon as she was mobile and well again, she disregarded the doctor's advice to rest every afternoon and set off for Huddersfield at least twice a week, where she would meet her friends and enjoy tea at Heywood's Café. Inevitably, within a couple of years she suffered another stroke. I remember Mam saying, as she resumed the heavy burden of caring for her, that some days she would just get her hands into the pastry and she would hear the call.

'Connie'.

'Yes, Mother, what is it?'

'Just come here a minute'.

So, she would clean her hands and go upstairs.

'Yes, Mother, do you want the commode?'

'No. I just wanted to look at you, love'.

It was all very difficult and exhausting. She did, however, give Mam the money to buy a washing machine which must have helped enormously.

Sometimes Mam would arrive home after shopping to find Grandma laid across the bed, false teeth out and the pillow on the floor. She was going to get out of bed and walk! The pillows were there to cushion her fall.

The doctor tried to persuade her to go into Deanhouse Hospital. He could see Mam was almost at breaking point, but she had it firmly fixed in her mind that Deanhouse was still the old workhouse, as it had been in her youth. No way was she going into the workhouse. The shame and the humiliation were unthinkable! How could it even be mentioned, never mind considered seriously! Eventually the truth prevailed with her, perhaps she could see how exhausted Mam had become, and she consented to go. It must have been a relief to Mam, although the bus journey to Netherthong and the long walk from there to the hospital must have been both time consuming and tiring. To the last, this fiercely independent lady insisted she could walk and that she did her five finger exercises every day, under the covers. Her strength and determination were incredible and I'm sure she lived on sheer will-power for a long time, but these undoubted qualities made her a very difficult patient indeed.

I think Grandma's strokes, or seizures, as they were referred to, affected me very deeply. To see Grandma, this energetic, smart, active lady reduced to a bedridden helpless invalid was cruel. She was paralysed down one side and her poor useless hand had to be moved for her, to place it under the bedclothes. When Mam sat her up on her pillows, she sagged over to one side, unable to keep in a sitting position. She was never a cuddly person, all the fun and the hugs and the stories had come from Grandad, but I loved her and the distress persisted, giving me nightmares, and a deep dread of suffering such an affliction myself.

Figure 3.5
Grandma and Grandma Wagstaff with Connie, my mother.

Little girls are notoriously curious about the contents of drawers and I was no exception. I can remember going up to the big bedroom at Ivy Cottage and quietly opening Grandma's drawers. There were pretty silk scarves that I had never seen used, small round cardboard pill boxes containing rouge and face powder, and small pots of Ponds Cold Cream, and astonishingly, Ponds Vanishing Cream! I remember gingerly putting some on my hand, and waiting... Was it relief or disap-

pointment when nothing happened? There were small
stubs of eyebrow pencil, one end brown, the other black,
and no lipstick. There were pretty diamante brooches
which clipped on to the neck of a dress, and lavender flowers scattered in the bottom of the drawer, lending their
faint sweet scent to everything. There were hair pins in
a box, long fancy hat pins, and something like a long soft
sausage made of hair with which Grandma had achieved
her bouffant hair styles, carefully combing her thinning
hair over the padding and fixing it in place with the hair
pins or a hair net. There were strings of beads and pearls,
long dangling ear-rings, some of which I still have, and
tablets of wallflower scented soap. She was a proud lady
and she and Grandad must have made a fine couple. He
had wavy hair and a moustache. He used to twist the ends
of the moustache with a perfumed wax, and always wore
a flower from the garden in his buttonhole. Their home
was a little palace and their garden a park!

Grandad's reputation as a painter and decorator
was second to none and as a child I became accustomed to
friends of my Mother telling me that '....your Grandfather
always did our decorating and the graining on the doors
is beautiful. I could never bear to have it painted over. No
one could do it like him!'

I was somewhat taken aback when I recently met
a group of people from Holmfirth and at the age of fifty-
seven, was told again about Grandad's painting! '...and of
course', said the lady who remembered him so clearly, 'he
would never tell you how long it would take. It'll get as
long as it needs, he would say, and when he went to the
toilet, you never knew how long that would take either,
he'd take the newspaper, or his cigarettes, or both!'

He was also known for his sense of humour, always full of fun and mischief. His tall stories were told with such serious conviction that you really didn't know whether to believe him.

Nosiness was, and probably still is, endemic in a small place like Underbank. People would stand at their doors and watch the 'goings on' and gossip; curtains would twitch as the hidden watchers kept an eye on things, and the social life thrived.

The lady who lived next door to Ivy Cottage was rumoured to keep a duster handy on the chair beside the front door, so that if she heard anyone coming, she could pick it up quickly and go out to shake it, thereby discovering who was passing, where they came from and who they were visiting. One day, when Grandad was at home from work recovering from the flu, he decided to put the rumour to the test. Grandma had gone to Holmfirth shopping and he was alone. Now the house next door was a little way in front of Ivy Cottage, so that to see our visitors, the lady had to be right out of her door and had to turn to look. Grandad took his walking stick, very quietly opened the front door and with the stick he reached out and rattled the gate catch, then nipped smartly back indoors and to the window. Sure enough, out she came, gallantly shaking her duster. No one was to be seen, so in she went. Again, after a few minutes, he rattled the gate, and again she appeared with the duster, shaking it vigorously. He had a very entertaining afternoon until Grandma returned. When he told her what he'd been about she was very cross, but they had a good laugh together and the events of that afternoon were a source of delight for many a long day, especially as the lady concerned tried to 'pump' information out of Grandma. She was obviously consumed with curiosity about the unseen visitors!

He and Dad got on very well and this in all probability influenced Mam to marry Dad. She adored her father. She learnt too late that a person who is extremely good company in public is not always such good company in private. She would say to me, 'You never know what goes on when that front door is shut'.

Of Grandma's family I know very little. There were, I think, some cousins who lived in Honley, and Auntie Lily, her sister, who lived in Blackpool. I clearly remember visiting her. She was married to a man called Law Denny and they had a daughter, Rona. Auntie Lily was small boned, pretty and rather like Grandma about the eyes. Uncle Law was short, rather coarsely featured, and somewhat coarsely spoken. Mam was very fond of crab, but he put her off it forever when he told her that when people are drowned, the crabs eat all the 'nangnails'. No wonder! Ugh! They were, I think, caretakers at the Municipal Offices and lived in a flat on the premises, but when Uncle Law retired, or left that job, they moved into a house with Rona and her husband Jack, who was a stoker on the railway. Rona and Jack had one half of the house, Auntie Lily and Uncle Law the other. I recall Mam being very upset when Auntie Lily became ill, feeling no one really looked after her. After her death, Uncle Law took to his bed and lived for many years as an invalid in spite of being in good health!

Another sister of Grandma's was Auntie Mary, married to Uncle Percy in Leeds, and they had one son, Gordon. He married a tall, dark-haired lovely girl called Blossom, and brought her to visit us at Ivy Cottage. She was a city girl, fashionable and glamorous, and glamour was in short supply in Underbank. I remember Mam being shocked at her platform-soled shoes! Blossom was a

Jewess, and while we were very aware of the large Jewish community in Leeds, to actually welcome someone of the Jewish faith into the family was an exciting event. Auntie Mary's house was called Kismet, which means Fate, and this seemed quite sinister when she discovered she had a growth on her leg, and hanged herself in the stairs

These are the only relations of Grandma Wagstaff's that I can recall, but I am sure there were many more in Holmfirth. Maybe her marriage to Fred had caused too serious a breach with her family.

The Wagstaff family, however, were prolific and the name crops up repeatedly throughout the Valley. Grandad came from a large branch of the family, Beatrice, Phoebe, Daniel, Beaumont and several more, and they all lived in Underbank until their respective marriages or other circumstances took them away. Uncle Beaumont, in particular, moved far away. He was the black sheep of the family, so the tale goes. He got a girl 'into trouble' and refused to marry her. In those days, breach of promise was an offence, punishable by law, and he departed the area as a wanted man! Rumour has it that the child was the very image of him ,of course!

Uncle Dan lived in Richmond, in North Yorkshire, although I don't remember him as he died comparatively young, like Grandad. I do remember lovely holidays in Richmond with Auntie Grace, his widow. Richmond is a delightful small country town, with a cobbled square, and at that time, no fewer than thirteen pubs! Or so I was told! The castle is wonderful, towering above the River Swale, and the walls were hung with wild flowers that I had never seen before: ivy-leaved toadflax, valerian, pennywort, lichens and mosses, ranging in colour from bright yellow through green to grey and almost white. It was a joy to look them up in my little book and identify them. The views from the battlements were superb, and the feeling that people had lived there hundreds of years ago, kept watch through the narrow windows, patrolled the battlements, was quite magical. I think it must have been the very first castle I had ever visited.

Auntie Grace was a dear, and lived just on the outskirts of the town, quite near to the river. To me, the Swale was a 'real' river, wide and deep, fast flowing and thrilling. It made me realise that our rivers, the Holme and the Ribble, were little more than moorland streams! At night, when the river was in spate you could hear the rushing water as you dropped off to sleep. There was a series of waterfalls just across the field from the house, and at low water you could cross over on the boulders, but when the river was high, the force and the roar were tremendous. I remember one year looking with amazement at the line of sticks and debris that lay ten or fifteen yards from the bank, revealing just how high the water had been.

Perhaps the most enduring memories of Auntie Grace's bow-windowed, semi-detached house are its nearness to the river, the smell of a scented geranium which she grew in a pot in the sitting room, and the monster of a water softener in the kitchen, which, if memory serves me right, had to be fed with quantities of salt! It never seemed to work. The water remained as hard and unresponsive to soap as ever.

Auntie Grace's son, Ken and his wife Eleanor lived in the town and their two youngest children were Kenny, just a bit older than me and Linda, just a bit younger. It was grand to have their company, to mess about in the river together, and walk for miles along the bank and through the woods. There was a very small church some distance away along the bank, St. Agatha's, and occasionally our walks took us there. We would climb over the stile into the graveyard, read the gravestones and the church notices, especially the rather gruesome story of her martyrdom. It was a gloomy place; the trees cut out much of the sunlight and made it feel quite eerie. At other times we went into the town, and to the church where Kenny was in the choir. We admired the lovely carvings, which had been done by a local wood carver, Robert 'Mousey' Thompson, who carved a small mouse somewhere on each piece of his work, as his trade mark or signature. It was fun to see if we could find them.

One night when we had all gone to bed, and the summer night through the bay window was dark and velvety, I lay listening to the sound of the river and gently dropping off to sleep, when I heard a different noise. Mam heard it too, a whispering kind of noise, a rustling, maybe a mouse, or a bird, in the room. Mam put on the light, and there was a dark bird-like creature flying round and round the room, clumsily now, bumping into the light, the curtains, the chimney breast. Mam took a towel and wafted at it until finally she hit it and it fell stunned to the floor. It was a bat! Perhaps it had come down the chimney, or through the open window, but, alas, it was dead now. The small furry body was much like a mouse and the wings, with the elongated fingers to support them, were enormous in comparison, and very delicate. After our laughter and the excitement we felt very sad that the episode had ended with the animal's death. Had we but thought, we could have left the light out, and most probably the bat would have found its own way out into the night. So sad that so often the only chance we have of examining such wonderful creatures is when they have accidentally been killed.

Of course, visits to Richmond were few and far between, but the happiness they brought makes them stand out like jewels in my memory.

Much nearer home were Grandad's sisters, Beatrice and Phoebe. Auntie Beattie (to be accurate, my Great Aunt Beatrice) lived in Underbank with her husband.

Looking back now, there was an abundance of quaint and eccentric names among the older people! His name was Battye Armitage. Auntie Beattie and Uncle Battye had one daughter, Joan, who is about fourteen years older than me. Their house had been the family home when Grandad was a lad. It was one of the curiously designed houses which cling to the

Figure 3.6
Aunt Beatie
with Joan, as a baby

hillside; apparently it was a conventional two storey terrace house in Dunford Road, but go down the steps at the end of the terrace, through the ginnel to Low Side, and there, directly underneath their house was another two storey dwelling, which also belonged to them. From the back, therefore, the house appeared to have four storeys! When Joan married Sidney Kippax, they moved into the little house on Low Side. Their sons Paul and David were born there, and later, when their daughter Anne came along, they moved up to the house on the main road which had three bed-rooms, and Auntie Beat and Uncle Battye moved to Low Side.

They were great 'curtain-twitchers', and knew the movements of everyone in Underbank - the eyes and ears of the world! They had a tiny garden in which Auntie Beattie always grew calceolarias (bright yellow flowers which had the appearance of a small pouch. I thought them wonderful!). There always seemed to be the faintest whiff of camphor in their house, and their light fitting had glass 'icicles' hanging from it. I thought it quite beautiful and longed for Mam to have one like it.

Auntie Beattie could have quite a sharp tongue. I remember Mam used to say she could curl her lip in disgust! What at, I don't know, but Mam was a gentle soul and would be no match for a sharp tongued Aunt. She also had the somewhat undignified ability to 'rift' or break wind at will, and there were times when Mam or Dad was suffering from indigestion that they were quite envious of this gift! It seemed a strange accomplishment to me, who was brought up to do such things very discreetly, if at all!

Uncle Battye was always very fond of Mam, and he used to pop in to Ivy Cottage quite often. He had been wounded during the Great War, and left for dead on the battlefield of the Somme. He recovered, but lived his life with a very thick boot and a serious limp. If you put a hand into his trouser pocket, so Mam said, you realised that almost half of his pelvis had been blown away. It was a miracle he survived. He worked at Cuttle Mill, just above the village, as a weaver. He must have been very strong indeed to have coped with such a physically demanding job with his disability. Eventually, of course, it became too much for him and he retired.

I can see him now, toiling laboriously along Kippax Row to visit us, determined to keep going at all costs. I still think of him on Remembrance Day, although he has been gone these many years. Mam was still quite a young girl when the First World War ended, and with all the tactlessness of the young, asked him if he had ever killed anyone. He replied that at one time he had three Germans on his bayonet and the third said to the

Figure 3.7
Grandad Wagstaff in the First World War

55

others 'move up a bit, I'm falling off!' With such grim humour did the brave soldiers retain their sanity! Uncle Battye also obliged when our little dog Wendy had a litter of
pups. She was only small and Mam felt that three were
too much for her. She told this to Uncle Battye and said
what should she do? He took the smallest pup and went
into the wash kitchen and drowned it in the washing water! Mam was taken aback at this apparent callousness,
but remarked that Wendy did not seem to miss the third
puppy, to which Uncle Battye commented 'Well, she can't
count, can she?

Grandad Wagstaff also went to France, but not to
the Somme. He was a driver in the Transport Core, and
part of his job was to carry away the dead bodies of the
men who fell victim to the terrible 'flu epidemic. He and
his mate never caught the 'flu, because, he said, they spent
every night in their hut eating raw buck onions! The smell
must have been quite something; you could cut the air
with a knife, but it protected them from the infection.

I was sent to stay with Auntie Beattie and Uncle Battye when Grandad Wagstaff died. I had never slept away
from home without Mam before, and I can clearly remember the small bedroom in their house. There was an alarm
clock with a luminous dial, and figures of gnomes digging
to every tick tock of the hands. Not being much of a dolly
person, I had been persuaded to take one with me. She
was called Mary and had a red knitted dress. I never really liked her; she was no comfort to me. I wonder why I
didn't take my teddy bear, which was much loved. Perhaps it had been left behind at our house in Huddersfield,
and Mary was the only doll available. When I was finally
taken back to Ivy Cottage, I ran, full of my news, up the
stairs to tell Grandad about the wonderful clock, and there

was the bed, neatly made, the counterpane smooth and unblemished. No Grandad. The desolation of that moment strikes me now, as I write.

All the memories of him are warm and happy, simple loving memories, of him taking me down the garden to the greenhouse and lifting me up so that I could pick the small ripe tomatoes and eat them, there and then, looking with him at the chrysanthemums in the Autumn, and being taken to the Underbank Flower Show where he won so many prizes. He would take me by the hand and we would climb the steep winding stairs at the Working Men's Club into the Show Room and the warm damp sweet scent would surround us. He would sit with me before bed in the little brown leather armchair with the velvet cushions and read stories and look at books. Sometimes we even looked at wallpaper pattern books together, right through from the very expensive papers that were gilded and heavily embossed to the cheap thin papers at the end. I would love to find the children's patterns, with animals, and one with, I think, 'Little Black Sambo' printed on it. He died at the age of sixty-six when I was seven years old. During that difficult time, I knew nothing of the pain and anguish until it was all over, thanks to the love and care of Auntie Beattie and Uncle Battye.

Auntie Phoebe, Grandad's other sister, also married a man with a quaint name, Friend Mellor. Uncle Friend was a jolly little man, as I recall, but Auntie Phoebe was the dominant character. Grandad called her, 't Wasp'! They had three daughters, I think, only one can I remember. She was Auntie Cissie and she and Uncle Tommy had a daughter Joan who was about my age, but lived in Clayton West, a long distance away. They would occasionally visit us, and Joan and I spent a happy time mixing up bits of this and that from the greenhouse in a jar, silver sand, potash, sulphate of ammonia, whatever we could find! It always turned out brown and disgusting. We never suffered any harm from this, but I can't imagine young children being allowed to play with such things, unattended, nowadays. Come to think of it, maybe we weren't allowed to then, and it was even more fun because it was forbidden, and secret.

Mam would sometimes take me to see Auntie Phoebe on a Sunday afternoon. I would sit by the fire where there was a little bookcase, and look at all the books in turn Sunday afternoon. I would sit by the fire where there was a little bookcase, and look at all the books in turn Eventually I found one which attract-

Figure 3.8
Auntie Phoebe with her three daughters, looking somewhat dazed. Imagine the effort that went into preparing the dresses curling their hair with ringlets and making them sit still, so as not to spoil the effect!

ed me. It was very old, even then, and it was the song of 'The Tailor and the Mouse', with pictures.

There was a tailor had a mouse, Ay diddle um cum feedle,
They lived together in one house, Ay diddle um cum feedle,
Ay diddle um cum tarum tantrum,
Through the town of Ramsey,
Ay diddle um cum over the lea,
Ay diddle um cum feedle.

The tailor thought the mouse was ill,
He gave him half of a blue pill.
Ay diddle...etc

The tailor thought the mouse would die,
He baked him in an apple pie.
Ay   diddle...etc.

Quite where I found or heard the tune of this little ditty, I don't remember, but I used to sing it, piercingly, to annoy Mam!

Auntie Phoebe's house was full of furniture, you could hardly move in their living room, or so it seemed to me, but aside from this I have no real personal recollections of them. One occasion I do remember. On their Golden Wedding, their family hired a coach and we all went off on a trip to Sherwood Forest and the Dukeries, and took the splendid celebration cake with us! A golden day indeed! Another memory was when two of their daughters wanted to get married, and planned to have a double wedding. It was March and many couples chose to marry then in order to claim back a whole year's income tax, but of course, it is also Lent, and the Vicar would not allow a double marriage, so the weddings were held separately, on successive weeks. it must have increased the cost substantially.

These are the only blood relations that I can recall, and much of my knowledge of them came from my Mother. All were considerably older than I, except for the cousins in Richmond and Clayton West , much too far away ever to be close friends. Nevertheless, I retained, and still do to some extent, a sense of belonging, of roots going deep, of fibres woven intricately into the fabric of life. I remember them all with affection, and they contributed a sense of family to my life, an extended family.

CHAPTER FOUR

Early Days and School Days

My earliest memories are not of Holmfirth, however, but of the house in Huddersfield where my parents lived after their marriage. It was a terrace house with a passage leading to the back yard. It must have been a very inconvenient house to run. There were two bedrooms on the top floor, a sitting room at street level, and a cellar kitchen, lit by a window half below the ground and covered with a grating. It must also have been something of a culture shock to Mam, moving from a very small town, surrounded by moors and countryside, from a cottage with a garden and a bathroom, to a town terrace with a back yard and an outside lavatory.

We lived mostly downstairs in the cellar kitchen, as to have lit two fires would have been extravagant and wasteful. Everything had

Figure 4.1
Dad in the R.A.F.

had to be used sparingly in war time, and coal was no exception. Consequently the rest of the house was very cold. I can only once remember having a fire in the sitting room and that was when I had whooping cough and my cot was brought there from the bedroom, making things easier for Mam. I remember very clearly lying in my cot and looking through its bars at the fire. I also vaguely remember being taken to where the road was being repaired in order for me to breathe in the tar fumes, so good for whooping cough!

I also recall lying in my cot in the bedroom and hearing the siren, and being taken downstairs in the middle of the night into the passage which served as air-raid shelter, and had a great iron door at each end. I thought this was very exciting, but I can't imagine my enthusiasm was shared! Huddersfield was pretty safe from bombing; the only worthwhile target being the ICI works which, in the scale of things, was relatively small. However, the sound of air planes droning overhead was common enough. Sheffield and Rotherham, with their steel-works were a mere thirty miles away.

Dad was away in the RAF, and at about thirty-eight or forty years of age was among the last and the oldest men to be called up. Mam had to take in an evacuee, as did anyone with a spare bedroom. Rather to her relief, this proved to be an elderly cockney gentleman, Mr Hiscock.

Many people had to take in women and children, and this caused not a few problems, two women in the kitchen, differing tastes and habits, extra children to feed, it all contributed to stress, quarrels and bad feeling. Mr Hiscock, however, was a gentle, quiet old man, who rather took over the role of Uncle for me. He had worked as a docker in the East End of London, and arrived straight from days and nights spent in the Underground, sheltering from the Blitz. It must have been a shocking experience, knowing it was unlikely you would see your home again; the walls of the Underground Station running with condensation, old and young cooped up together, listening to the noise of bombs falling. I think he truly 'landed on his feet' when he arrived at Mam's door. She took him in, fed him and looked after him. He used to take me for walks in the nearby Victoria Park and when I re-visited it only a few years ago, I instantly recognised the monkey-puzzle tree, the huge pine tree where we used to pick up the needles and the strange forbidding rocks where there is still a kind of cave which used to frighten me.

Figure 4.2
Mr. Hiscock, our evacuee,
at home in Plaistow.
He is the white-haired gentleman on the right

One day we set out on our walk armed with an empty matchbox in which to put any interesting creature we found, maybe a 'woolly boy' caterpillar, or a ladybird, or a shiny beetle. As so often happens when you go prepared, we found nothing, and we were returning home empty handed and disappointed, when we saw a fat slug in the grass. At last, a creature to take home! Into the matchbox he went and we returned triumphant. Of course, after all that searching for caterpillars we were late for tea, so the matchbox was placed carefully on top of my books in my little chair.

The next day, I remembered the slug and eagerly went to find it. No matchbox! Not on the chair, not on the floor, where could it be? Mam had come upon it after I had gone to bed, and protruding from

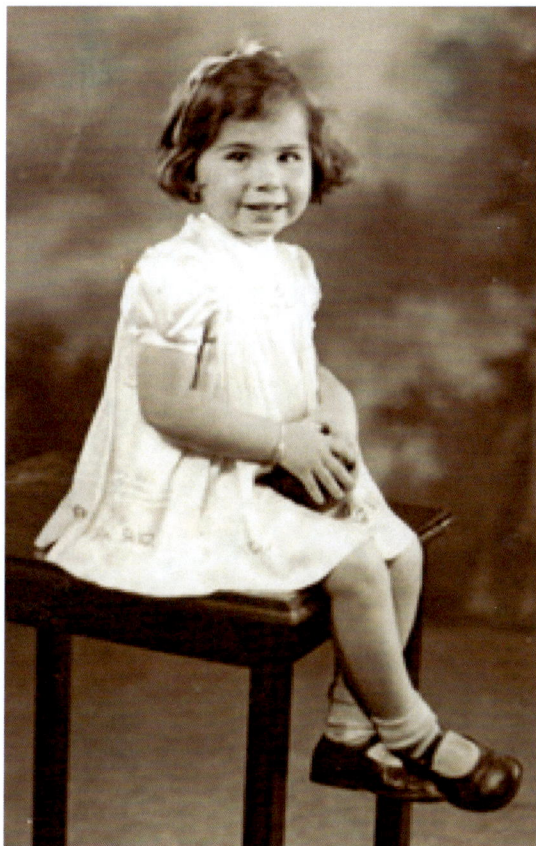

Figure 4.2
Christine at
3 years old.

from the end were the two large horns and part of its head! In horror, the matchbox, complete with slug, was dumped unceremoniously in the dustbin! I was so upset, and we were both told off severely!

One of the neighbours in Mount Street, directly across the road, had a pet monkey, and now and again, Mam would take me over to see it. It was quite small, with a blue 'waistcoat', and would chitter away at us, and leap from chair to table to sideboard, and up the curtains like lightning! It was called Billy. I was a teeny bit afraid of it, and I can't remember ever being allowed to hold it, which is probably just as well, as on one occasion, it bit Mam's leg quite badly. It couldn't have been much of a life for a monkey, in a small terrace house with a cellar kitchen.

At about this time, I had my first experience of being left with a group of children of about my own age, which must have been three or four. As an only child, I was much more accustomed to the company of adults, and this experience left its mark. I can only suppose it was a crèche where Mam left me to do some Christmas shopping, but it proved a shattering blow to my self-esteem! Amongst all these children, hurtling around on

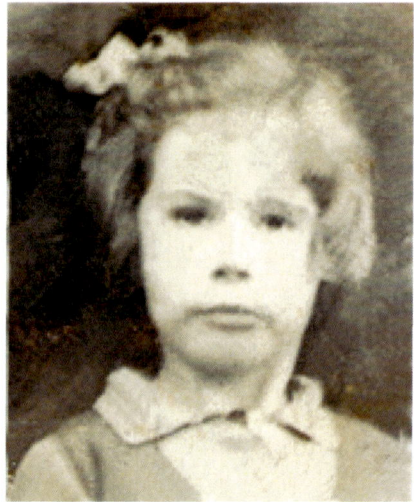

Figure 4.3
Christine at 5 years of age, first school photo

tricycles, the noise of shouting and laughing, I didn't know what to do, didn't know anyone.

At length, a boy came charging up and offered me a ride on his bike. I laughed and laughed hysterically and uncontrollably because I couldn't quite manage to get on, and then, horror of horrors, I felt my knickers grow wet and a large puddle appeared on the floor! The boy rode off and I was left standing there, and then Mam arrived. I cried and cried with relief, shame, anguish and humiliation. I was never left again.

The War, in fact, did not encroach on my consciousness very much. The sirens and the air planes were just an exciting part of life; Mr Hiscock was just another person to play with and talk to, but at the crossroads near the shops, I came to understand some of the fear that war engendered. While we were shopping one day, there seemed to be lots more people about than usual, and then we heard a terrible grinding, roaring noise. Round the corner came a convoy of tanks, their size, and menacing lack of windows, or 'eyes', or any glimpse of humanity, terrified me! The huge caterpillar treads left deep marks in the surface of the road and right up on to the pavement. I was shocked and scared and clung on to Mam; the tracks were still there the next time we went shopping! To this day, tanks fill me with dread. Apart from playing with the little boys with their Tommy Guns and their mocking, 'Heil Hitler' salute, one finger laid across the top lip for the famous moustache, the other hand up in the air, that was all the War that I was aware of.

In 1945, at the end of the war, Mr Hiscock returned to London, to his own family. It was with sadness that we said goodbye, with many promises to keep in touch.

Life continued along its uneventful way for me,

until at last, at long last, the great day arrived; the day when I was to start school, when I would learn to read and write! I had looked forward to it for ages and now, on a sunny September morning I set out with Mam for Mount Pleasant School. Most of my friends in the street had already started school, and Shirley, who lived opposite us, now had glasses! I was filled with admiration for the glasses and maybe when I went to school, I would have some too! There was little preparation for such an enormous change in life, beyond parents telling children they must put up their hand when they wanted to speak, and to be good, or you might finish up wearing a dunce's hat!

I'm not at all sure what I expected that first day to be like, but certainly not the crowds of children, all pushing and shoving, and several cross-sounding teachers trying vainly to put us in orderly queues! Amongst all this confusion, to my alarm, I desperately needed the toilet. Someone pointed me in the right direction, and when I returned I found myself in a different queue and we were quickly marched off into a classroom. Miss Whiteley called out everyone's name, except mine. So she added mine to her list, and when someone came in and asked if Christine Strange was with her, she just replied yes, and I stayed. I discovered later that I had actually arrived in the second class! Not bad, to be moved up on your first day!

Mam fetched me at dinner time and I never stopped talking all through our meal. When she put on her coat to take me back for the afternoon, I became really upset. I wanted to go by myself! I didn't need her to take me! What a cocky child I must have been! So, the compromise was made, Mam took me down the hill, saw me safely across the road, and I continued on my own.

I loved Miss Whiteley. She was tall and slim, with freckles, and I thought she was wonderful, even when I was made to stand in the corner, a frequent punishment for talking. I remember the frustration and the humiliation. I remember examining in great detail the wood panelling and its many different pinholes! I was also punished sometimes by being made to sit in the front desk beside Billy. Billy was a bit slow, not altogether clean, and I hated that.

It was all very formal, we sat side by side, in our double desks, pencils had to be handed in each day, and given out again next morning, and oh the joy of being given that little job, and being sure of having a long, new pencil, with a sharp point! The only lesson I can remember was when we were told about 'Ship half-pennies' and how the words 'Ind Imp' no longer appeared on our coinage, because our monarch is no longer Empress of India. Lessons in general I loved, but playtime, that was another matter entirely. Playtime, I hated. I can only recall being cold and miserable, huddled up against the wall or under the long shelter. Although I had played happily with the other children in Mount Street, I can't remember them at school at all, not even Shirley with her new glasses. One friend I can recall. She was called Jean Spooner, and she was plump and had long fair fat ringlets, and was fun. With her I felt safe.

Having established my independence on my first day, I was allowed to walk to and from school by myself, Mam looking out for me at the appropriate time, I suppose. One day, after school, I walked with Jean all along Victoria Road; she wanted me to visit her house, but when we reached the road junction, panic set in and I realised that if I went any further

I would be lost, so we said goodbye and I retraced my steps. It seemed very lonely along the road, no one about and the unmistakable feeling of being late. However, our conversation had been about walnuts for some reason, and logically, I thought that if walnuts were so called, they must be found growing in walls! All the way back home, I searched in all the crevices of the wall, and, of course, found nothing. I was so disappointed and felt rather cheated. However, it must have taken some of the steam from Mam's anxiety when she heard my tale, after all, I was very late! I was told not to be so silly, and not to do such a thing again, and then she laughed at my foolishness.

That was not my only misconception. We often went shopping together, and there at the crossroads, were traffic lights. These featured strongly in our lives, Mam explaining that I must wait until the lights were red for the traffic before it was safe to cross. Standing there with her, looking at the black and white striped post, I thought what a very thin man he must be, the man who switched the lights from red, to amber, to green!

When I was about eight, we moved to Holmfirth and Ivy Cottage. Grandma was not well and Mam felt she must be there to care for her, and when she suffered a stroke, Mam's hands were very full indeed. It must have been a very difficult time for Mam, worried about Grandma, Dad not wanting to leave Huddersfield and me to look after. How were they ever to get all the furniture from two households into the small rooms? Grandma and Grandad had a lovely home, but difficult compromises must have had to be made. No wonder she had little time for me.

What did I do with myself during the brief weeks while Mam and Dad were sorting out our lives and organ

-ising the move? No school, no friends or other children around; they were at their school, of course. I was able to read by this time, and I read and re-read my books. I helped Mam, went shopping with her, ran errands, and 'helped' in the house. About that time, I seem to remember, she taught me to knit. Perhaps I had a knitting-set for Christmas, and I struggled manfully to master the art. The number of stitches seemed to vary mysteriously with each row, and they were so tight on the needle I could hardly get the other needle in to knit a stitch! Now and again a small hole would appear. My hands grew hot and sweaty from holding the needle so tightly, and Mam had to keep sorting me out. My other time-filling occupation was to 'go for a walk', when Mam was at her wit's end. I imagine the conversation went something like this-

> 'What can I do?'
> 'Read your book.'
> 'I've read a book.'
> 'Well, read another book.'
> 'Don't want to.'
> 'Well, go for a walk.'
> 'I've been for a walk.'
> 'Well, go again, a different way'.

In fact, I spent many happy hours exploring the lanes, the woods and the little river, finding and identifying wild flowers in the little book Cousin Kenneth had given me, a book I still have, and still use! Such freedom was wonderful, and mostly, I loved it. I cannot imagine a little girl being allowed to wander the countryside alone nowadays, even in Underbank! The world was a safer place then, but Mam must have been very relieved when I was able to start school again, and life became organised once more. Eventually, I started attending school in Holmfirth.

It was very much smaller than Mount Pleasant, and was still referred to as the National School by almost everyone.

My first teacher there was Mrs Battye, who had taught my mother before me! She was short and round and had three chins and a loud commanding voice. Occasionally, she would address me as Constance, when I was chattering. I knew she meant me, and the message was 'stop talking', but I would pretend I didn't know who she was talking to. My first friend there was called Auriol and we sat together, in a double desk, on the back row. Among other things, Mrs Battye taught us music, and used a tuning fork which I found quite perplexing. She would take this small metal instrument and hit it smartly on her desk, then stand it on its other end for us to hear the note! Amazing, like magic! We sang lots of songs with her, mostly traditional like 'The Bluebells of Scotland', and 'Annie Laurie', 'The British Grenadiers' and 'The Ash Grove'. I loved them all, it was great fun, and when one day, Mrs Battye announced we were to form a Percussion Band, I could hardly contain myself with excitement and anticipation. One of the other teachers came in to play the piano and we were all presented with instruments. To my great disappointment I was given a triangle. Not a drum or a tambourine, which seemed really exciting, but a triangle. What was worse, I only had to hit it twice in the whole performance and then I managed to do it at the wrong time! Mrs Battye also taught us the Tonic Sol-fa. She had a kind of scroll which she fixed to the top of the blackboard and it hung down, revealing the magic code of Doh, Ray, Me and so on. She stood beside it with a wooden stick and we had to sing the note as she pointed to it. I was always wrong! Alas, these lessons revealed me to be a lover of music, but no musician at all! I hated that lesson and I dreaded it coming around.

In the interests of our health, we had regular visits from the School Nurse, who, I think, weighed us, measured us, and checked our hair for nits. We were also visited by the dentist. I did not require any treatment while I was at National School and I confess I was quite disappointed. As I had never endured the drilling and the filling, I knew no better. What interested me were the small blobs of quicksilver which the children who had fillings showed me. It was a magical, silvery liquid held in the palms of their hands. Sometimes it was a single round blob, and sometimes it broke up into several drops, only to meet together again as my friend half-closed her hand. It left no trace behind, no smudge, no wetness. It was magic and I was enthralled. Why couldn't I have some, too? The substance filled me with wonder; clearly the poisonous nature of mercury had not been realised in those days.

Rather more healthily, we had milk every day, in small third-of-a-pint bottles, which I wasn't too keen on, except in the winter when it often arrived frozen. That was good fun, prodding the mushy ice with a straw. Eventually it would melt sufficiently to be sucked up, and 'woe betide' anyone who made a gurgling sound when the milk was almost gone!

School dinners were good. We had mince quite often, stew, and sometimes winter salad, with shredded raw cabbage and carrot and beetroot. There were lovely sponge puddings with ginger or a bit of jam, and custard. Sometimes we had semolina and chocolate semolina, both of which I disliked and was made to eat! Very occasionally we were given a lovely red apple, a Mackintosh Red from Canada, and that was a real treat, white fleshed, sweet and delicious.

Sweets at playtime were a rarity, but sometimes we might have some Kay-lie, (sherbert) in a little pointed bag and we licked our finger and dipped it into the sweet lemony powder. It was very satisfying, especially when your finger turned bright yellow! Now and again we would take a little paper bag of cocoa and sugar to school, and again we licked our finger and dipped it into the tasty mixture.

I enjoyed school on the whole, except for Arithmetic which I hated and simply could not understand. By the time I was in the top class, Mr Rawlings' class, I was copying shamelessly from my friend Margaret's book, until she grew so far ahead that the pages had to be turned back to find the right place for me to copy! Margaret was a good friend and we spent a lot of time together. She visited at weekends and we played endless games of make-believe together. 'Our Game' we called it, re-enacting books we had read. Very occasionally we were taken to the pictures. We saw 'Treasure Island' there and found it so very exciting that it became a favourite. When Mam and I went to a Jumble Sale at Church I found a copy of the book, bought it, and read it all for myself. We also invented new names for ourselves, new families, lives of adventure.

School was not adventurous, it was strict and formal. Margaret and I shared a double wooden desk with an attached seat and an iron frame. There was only one lid, so you risked disturbing your friend's work if you needed to get something out which you had forgotten. We wrote with pens which we dipped into the inkwell, the nibs sometimes scratchy and twisted, sometimes thick and broad, and always with the danger of blots and smudges. Ink stained our fingers, our hankies and our clothes. It was a great privilege to be ink monitor and go round the desks filling up the small china inkwells, which were frequently filled with soggy ink stained blotting paper which had to be scooped out. What a messy job!

Playtimes and dinner times were spent in the school yard. In winter, the boys made long, long slides on the ice, terrifying to timid girls like me. We girls often played at skipping, sometimes individually and sometimes with a long rope, two of us to turn it. We would run in, skip, chanting the rhyme and then run out, or everyone would run in until there were three or four or even five of us skipping together. The rhyme we chanted mystified me.

'House to let,
A pie within,
When you go out
Mrs ...... comes in'

....and in you went when your name was called. It was a long time before I realised there was no pie, and the word was 'apply'! Balls were always good fun and we invented many variations on 'Catch' and 'Pig in the Middle'. Sometimes we were allowed to play with the hoops, swirling them round on our hips, 'Hula Hoops'. There were lots of games of 'Tig' and its variants were played by both girls and boys. One in particular I remember, called 'Den Relievo'. When you were caught by whoever was 'it', you had to go down to the small wall which separated the teacher's lavatory from the children's. There was a cranny there where the mortar had fallen away, and you had to put your hand in the gap and wait for someone to 'relieve' you from the 'den' by touching your hand. Of course, the complicated business of deciding who should be, 'it' took a long time too! We would 'dip' for it, putting up both up both fists and someone would touch them in turn, chanting,

> *'One potato, two potato, three potato, four,*
> *Five potato, six potato, seven potato more'.*

On the word 'more', that hand went behind your back and the whole process continued until only one hand was left - you were 'it'. Alternatively we chanted

> *Ickle, Ockle, chocolate bottle,*
> *O U T spells out',*

….and out you went; the last remaining one was, 'it'.

Whips and tops were popular in the cold weeks leading to Easter, and we spent a lot of time colouring our tops with chalk, experimenting with different patterns and colour combinations, fascinated by the way the colours merged as the top spun round faster and faster. I had a particularly good whip which Grandad had made for me. It had a stout wooden handle with my initials CMS scorched on to it with the poker, and a thick leather thong to which I attached about six inches of string. You had to wind the string, the 'lash,' around the top and pull the whip away very sharply to set the top spinning. It was all very technical and the preparations were often as enjoyable and time consuming as the game. You needed to find a good place too, as a pavement with nicks between the slabs, or with rough stony places, was no good; the top would not spin. Undoubtedly, the school yard with its smooth surface was the best place.

We also played 'Our Game' a lot. I gathered two or three other girls who were on the same make-believe wavelength, and found a little place, just round the corner from the main playground. When we heard the bell at the end of playtime, we would wait until all was silent, and then say 'OH' in loud disappointed tones, just to let anyone who cared to listen know that we didn't want to go back to our lessons!

From time to time, of course, as at the first school I attended, I was punished for talking, and was sent to the furthest part of the classroom, away from everyone. Not quite 'in the corner', staring at the panelling, but often reduced to reading the warning poster about Colorado Beetles which ate our potato crop, and longing to find one to claim the reward!

Perhaps the nearest thing to adventure was the day when a whole group of us decided to sneak out at dinner time and walk down into Holmfirth. This was strictly forbidden and we felt very daring as we walked along. Margaret was there, Beryl, Jean, Olwynne, Victor and Tony, I remember. We crossed the Square, went down the narrow strip of waste ground and so to the river. We were never allowed to play in the river because of the pollution from the mills and dye works, the water was often a dark muddy grey, the swarf and shreds of wool in the water coating the boulders and stones, but running water is always fascinating. It splashed and rippled over the stones, creating whirls and eddies, and over to the far bank a long deep pool had formed where the water hardly seemed to move. We laughed and shrieked with joy, stepping from stone to stone trying not to get our feet wet. It was such fun, so exciting, until Olwynne, who was standing on a boulder in the middle of the river, turned to call to us, slipped, and fell into the deep pool with a tremendous splash. A moment of silence followed, as we took in the catastrophe, then shouts and splashing as we tried to pull her out. She had gone right under, her hair was streaming, and her pretty pink and white striped dress clung to her hindering her as she vainly tried to get out, gulping and coughing. Thankfully, a man heard the commotion and came to the rescue. Quickly, she was pulled out of the filthy water, wrapped in a blanket, and her Dad summoned from the nearby butcher's shop where he worked. She was white faced, wet, tearful, sobbing, shivering, and she was whisked away from us. It was a very shame-faced and sober group of children who set off back to school, with the harsh words of the rescuer ringing in our ears. 'Supposing she had died', and 'it was all our fault!' That was just too awful to contemplate. What would Mr Rawlings say? Even worse, what would Mam say? 'Supposing Olwynne was not dead, but very, very ill...Supposing we were given the cane.... Supposing we were expelled....?'

Punishment was meted out swiftly. Our parents had to be told, and for the first and only time, I received a smart blow on each hand from Mr Rawlings' ruler. We all did. We were lined up and had to take our punishment. The pain, the shame, and the constant fear that maybe Olwynne was dead made that a most dreadful afternoon.

Olwynne was not dead, but she had several days off school until the doctor felt she was well enough to return, and the feared effects of the foul water, which she must have swallowed, were out of her system. She was quite a hero when she came back to us and basked in the glory, and so did the rest of us!

Life was good in Mr Rawlings' class, except for Arithmetic, of course, but my eleventh birthday was looming on the horizon, with the prospect of moving on to secondary education.

There was the exam to face which would decide my future, Grammar School, or Secondary Modern, which in those days provided no qualifications at all. Mam was anxious and begged Dad to pay for me to go to one of the private schools in Huddersfield, Fox's College, or Kay's College if I didn't pass, but Dad would have none of it. He was probably unable to find the money. The dreaded Arithmetic was the stumbling block as I always did well in English; my writing was good, legible and neat, and my spelling was good too, but the sums, oh dear, what about the sums?

Books were produced for me to look at, with problems for me to solve and mechanical exercises for me to practice. I dreaded the appearance of the book in the evening, but I can't say that it worried me exactly. I hated the problems; they always seemed to be about a man painting railings and being unable to decide how much paint he would need, or about someone filling a bath and how long it would take. These, and other similar questions, totally defeated me, and still do! After a few evenings of suffering, the book was abandoned, and life returned to its former relaxed and happy pattern.

The exam, however, could not be abandoned. Inevitably the day dawned, and I set off for Nabb School (the Secondary Modern) along with my friends. We had all been supplied with a pen with a new nib, and, as far as I can remember, a piece of blotting paper, a rare luxury indeed!

Nabb was across our valley, just out of sight of Ivy Cottage, over the brow of the hill. It was a good walk, over the bridge, up Swan Lane, past Swan Wood, which was carpeted with bluebells in May, and in early Spring we sought catkins and pussy willow.

Up Twisting Lane we went, over the stile and on to the road which would eventually have taken us to Holmfirth. Nabb was on this road. None of us had ever been there before and that fact, plus the impending exam, made us very apprehensive. It was slightly more modern than National School, but still had tall, high windows which you could not look out of, a playground, and ancient wooden desks complete with the precious inkwell. The wooden floors were noisy with the tramp of our feet and our anxious pushing and shoving. There were so many strange faces, children from every school in the area were there, and strange teachers telling us where to sit and to take out our pens. One child per desk, and the desks spaced out so no copying was possible. All the pictures hanging in the room had been turned to the wall, presumably to prevent us being distracted from our work. Actually, it made me wonder what the pictures could possibly have been that were thought to be so distracting, then the exam papers were handed out!

I cannot recall any of the questions, but I expect the luckless painter was there and the person running the bath. My new nib was very broad and inflexible and I didn't like what it did to my writing, but write I did, and went home singing and happy, totally unaware of the importance of the day.

Life continued on its pleasant path, books were read, compositions were written, paintings were painted and pictures were drawn, poems were learnt and games were played. Our class presented a play to the rest of the school in which I played the Sleeping Beauty. Margaret and I remained the best of friends and we became friends with the newest member of our class, Victor, who had the amazing accomplishment of 'singing' the Sabre Dance, with great energy and many vocal tricks. Victor was great fun and was the only boy to be introduced to 'Our Game'. Together we wrote a play which we were allowed to practice at lunch times in the Infants, downstairs. Olwynne was recruited and it changed with every rehearsal! It was called 'The Currant Bun' and involved Margaret being a ghost and wearing the rather worn piano cover as her costume. We had a wonderful time, and to our intense pleasure, Mr Rawlings said we could present it to the rest of the school. Olwynne brought the vital currant bun, and Margaret's Mum provided her with a real white sheet for her ghost part. This was the first disaster for the old piano cover was so thin that she was able to see through it quite easily, but the sheet allowed her no sight at all! Olwynne, at the right moment, took a bite of the bun and found she could not speak at all until she had chewed and swallowed it, an eternity, it seemed! Victor was required to make an entrance through a window, for which we used a free-standing blackboard which could be tilted or turned over as occasion demanded. He threw up the blackboard with great drama, and instead of staying horizontal so that he could climb through, it bounced on the top of my head and returned to the vertical! Well, we just dissolved into helpless giggles at that, and it was only with great difficulty that we completed our performance, but as everyone seemed to think it was meant to happen like that and everyone laughed and enjoyed it, perhaps it did not matter

The results of the exam came towards the end of the Summer Term, and I was not one of the two successful pupils. Alas, Holme Valley Grammar School was not for me. It was rumoured that there was to be a 'Second List' but the letter did not arrive until the first day of the holi holidays. I had passed the exam and was to start at

Penistone Grammar School in September! Mam and Dad were very thrilled, and so was I. What an adventure that was going to be!

It must have been some time that year that I started Elocu-tion Lessons with Miss Ella Hirst. I loved it! It was wonderful! I don't think Mam ever fully realised what a tremendous gift she handed to me when she bought me my hard backed exercise book and handed me my bus fare and three shillings fee each week. It gave me a life time of pleasure, which has grown with the years. After all, it was no good thinking of piano lessons, Grandma's piano had had to be sold, no good thinking of dancing class, Christine had no sense of rhythm, no good thinking of the Church Choir, for Christine could not sing in tune, but Elocution, a new poem every week, standing up and reciting it ; that was magic!

At my first lesson, I was asked if I knew any po-ems and could I recite one. I immediately remembered one I had discovered in an old Chatterbox Annual for 1917 which had belonged to Mam. It was a thick, heavy book, with double column printing, and all the illustrations were engravings, no colour at all. The poem was called 'Echoes' and mentioned Buenos Aires. I thought it wonderful and had learnt it by heart. I have wanted to visit Buenos Aires ever since then, such an exotic name for a place.
I think Mr Rawlings had realised my love of books and literature and when I presented him with my Autograph Book before I left National School, he wrote in it,

'The time has come' the Walrus said, 'to talk of many things.
Of shoes and ships and sealing wax, of cabbages and kings,
And why the sea is boiling hot, and whether pigs have wings'

I was thrilled and intrigued, and when I later discovered it in 'Alice through the Looking Glass,' I was delighted.

CHAPTER FIVE

No Place Like Home

Ivy Cottage was home. It was my mother's childhood home, where she was born, and it was my grandparents' home, and it was my home. It had low ceilings with beams, oak beams, which, according to Grandad, you could not hammer a six inch nail into as it would bend. There were stone-flagged floors and a stone sink in the corner which was hidden by cupboard doors; a large range heated both water and the oven.

Up the stone stairs to the landing, turn right and there was the most amazing bonus, a bathroom, again with a stone flagged floor, and a door leading directly into the top garden! Beyond the bathroom a wash kitchen, dimly lit from a small window set high in the wall, just below the ceiling. Very few of my friends had the luxury of an indoor toilet, never mind a whole bathroom. It was large and spacious, icy cold in winter, relieved only a little by opening the doors of the large cylinder cupboard, where Mam kept the sheets aired. Grandad had installed the bath and kept the surface painted, but for some reason, the water quickly became cold and you found yourself sitting on a cold spot. Years later, we discovered it was made of two inch thick stone! No wonder the water went cold under you, but nevertheless, it was a luxury. The room had the most wonderful acoustics, and I would sit and soap myself, singing loudly and exuberantly to myself, until one day, someone commented to Mam, who commented to me, that my singing could be heard on the top road. I found this very inhibiting, so my music making came to a stop.

Figure 5.1
Grandma at the door of Ivy Cottage

In the bathroom there was also a strange piece of furniture, two cupboards separated by a knee-hole, and a box standing on top. Was it a desk? Was it a wash stand? Who knows? It was always referred to as 'that piece of furniture in t'bathroom' It housed our small collection of remedies: Vaseline, Dettol, a bottle of Californian Syrup of Figs, lovely, a small bottle of Cascara, not so lovely, a bottle of Sloane's Liniment, bearing a picture of a heavily moustached gentleman from the Edwardian era, a small, rather sticky bottle of olive oil, for warming and putting in your ears in the event of earache, several round tubs made of cardboard containing Wintergreen Ointment for rubbing into sore joints , and a rather rusty tin of Kaolin Poultice, used for drawing pus out of boils, an extremely painful treatment, and something in a bottle called Fenning's Fever Cure, the dose of which you were directed to take in a wine glass. It was shockingly bitter and I would take almost an hour to swallow it even when Mam gave it to me in one of her best cut glass Sherry glasses.

Back through the small doorway and onto the landing again, with its creaky boards and the 'fixture wardrobe' which housed my clothes and shoes, my old dolls, two old dance dresses of Mam's and two swagger canes, one with a silver top and one with a parrot's head for a handle, often used for dressing-up games.

The small bedroom came first, with a fancy glass panel in the door, my bedroom. Under my bed was Grandad's old tin trunk with the initials F.W.H. on the lid (Fred Wagstaff, Holmfirth). Inside was a large brown paper parcel tied up with pink tape, containing the deeds of Ivy Cottage and the six cottages which had existed on what had become the garden. It was a very large parcel and when we opened it one day to have a look, we found large wide sheets of thick paper, covered in beautiful copper plate writing, almost impossible to read due to the legal language and the age of the documents which must have been dated about 1860.

Most of the floorboards creaked. I knew exactly how to avoid the noisy boards, but, being an old house, it had a presence of its own. I would lie awake and listen to the sighs and whispers and creaks of the old timbers; the distinctive smell was always there, greeting me as I came home from school, or more forcefully, when we returned from holiday. It was of lavender, polish, and Grandma's wallflower soap, with just a hint of mothballs.

On the landing was a very large photographic portrait of my Great Grandmother Wagstaff, looking very stern and wearing a little gold brooch which always lived in Mam's dressing table drawer. There was also a large photograph of Mam in her teens, unsmiling, but beautiful.

Mam and Dad's bedroom was further along the landing and was much bigger. It housed Grandma's huge mahogany wardrobe which had three sections, one a full-length mirror. It was equipped inside with drawers, hat-box, shoe space and hanging. It was absolutely wonderful, especially the mirror, and, of course, all Mam and Dad's new furniture!

Downstairs again to the living room or 'house', the heart of Ivy Cottage where meals were cooked and eaten, the baking and ironing, mending and sewing were done. There was also the sitting room, very grand and rather cold as it was mostly unused except when we had company, or at Christmas. Occasionally, Dad would take a shovelful of fire in there on a Sunday afternoon and we would enjoy the luxury of the lovely velvet three piece suite. Unfortunately, the chimney in there was rather eccentric, and often when the wind was in a certain quarter, the smoke from the fire would blow back, puffing gently into the room, making everything smell of soot and covering the hearth with tiny black flakes.

The house was where we lived and moved and had our being. It was warm and cosy and it had our constant companion in the corner, the wireless. It also contained another heirloom of Grandad's day. Between the stairs door and the pantry door stood a small chest of drawers, which, for some reason was always called the cupboards'; on top of this, stood Grandma's old clock, black and gilt with roman numerals, with a pillar on each side of the face.

Grandad and Grandma's presence gradually faded as Mam and Dad made Ivy Cottage their home.

Figure 5.2
The old range at Ivy Cottage was much like this. It was very efficient and served the family well, heating the room, the water and the oven

I well remember the day when the old range was taken out to be replaced by a tiled fireplace. This was a big step towards modernisation, no more black leading and polishing the brass fender! I came home from school to find the place in complete chaos. There was a tremendous, gaping hole in the wall almost to the ceiling. In the middle of the floor was a huge pile of bricks and rubble, and Mam was sitting on a chair, squashed up against the table at the back of the room. She was pale and worn and I think, had been crying. She had discovered that the diamond in her engagement ring was missing. How or why or where, she could not imagine. She had been wearing the ring, as she always did, a habit from the War when such valuables were kept on your person so that if the worst happened and you were bombed, at least you had something of value with you. Now, it was gone. She had sieved the washing water, examined all the dust and fluff in the vacuum cleaner, looked in the beds, in pockets, in the washing-up, everywhere. She was distraught! As we sat there, sunk in despair, her eye caught a glimpse of a twinkle on the floor, near the heap of rubble. It was the diamond! Unbelievably, it was found, in the midst of all the dirt! It felt like a miracle!

The following morning when the builders returned, they rejoiced too, and they wrote my initials, C M S in the new cement under the fire grate, where the diamond had so nearly been buried. I have that ring still, complete with that original stone. Now it gets worn only for special occasions!

Mam was, however, concerned that we would still be warm enough, but her fears were unfounded. Ivy Cottage faced a little bit South of West, so we had afternoon and evening sun. The stone walls were almost two feet

Figure 5.3 Ivy Cottage

thick, making it warm in winter and cool in summer.

It was not so cool in Summer as to keep the milk always sweet, though. Sometimes during a hot spell, Mam would boil the milk as soon as it arrived, to help keep it fresh longer. We said the milk was 'cracked' when that happened. It didn't taste too good either.

Meat was kept in a meat safe, a wooden cupboard on tall legs, with perforated zinc sides to allow free pas sage of cool air and keep the flies away. Jellies refused to set in the heat, even in the coolest part of the pantry; we did better than most, I think.

In winter we had no trouble keeping food fresh! Winters were long in Holmfirth and always, at some point, there was snow.

Oh the joy of walking along Kippax Row, making new footprints on the way to school, and especially good when the snow was so deep it came to the top of your 'wellies'. Fun, that is, until the snow fell inside the boot and your socks became wet and freezing cold.

We were always excited when we saw the huge snow plough go up Dunford Road to Hade Edge, or along the road up the Holme Valley towards the moors, clearing a way through to Holme village, and over the moors to Lancashire.

Folks would clear their paths and steps and then scatter the ashes from the fire to prevent people slipping on the ice. As no one had a car, there were no problems of that freezing up and refusing to start; the anxiety was that maybe the buses would not be able to get through. The fear of falling was uppermost in the minds of the elderly, and many old ladies, including Grandma, would put a pair of old socks over their shoes to give them a better grip. Interestingly, although Grandma, like everyone else was afraid of falling, she steadfastly refused to scatter ashes on our path, saying they trod into the house and made a mess!

Such times revealed the kindliness of people, who shovelled out the snow and cleared paths not only for themselves but for the elderly and infirm; they saw to the shopping, making sure that friends and neighbours were safe and warm, and well supplied with food.

Their kindliness was especially needed in the Winter of 1947 which was very severe, snow and ice for week after week, icicles hanging from roofs and drainpipes, impacted snow on the roads and footpaths, and higher up the hill great swaths of snowdrifts like the sand dunes of the desert, or like whipped cream, changing colour with the changing sky, tinged with pink at sunset in the late afternoon, grey and forbidding when the sky clouded and snow threatened yet again.

Figure 5.4 The view from Ivy Cottage

At Hade Edge the snow was up above the tops of the walls and the telegraph wires were so thickly coated with ice that they broke and drooped around the telegraph poles like giant maypoles. In such a winter, villages were cut off for weeks, electricity nonexistent. The birds were dying with the cold and the survivors came ever nearer to the houses where crumbs, cheese, bacon rind and other fatty morsels were left out for them.

In our top garden the trees were magical, so beautiful, like fairyland, and all the paths and rockeries were smoothed over, the steps disappeared. Mam took a photograph of the garden from the bathroom and when it was developed we discovered three sheep were there, up against the wall, eating the ivy! We had never noticed them, but there they were. How they got there, up the steep snow covered stone steps, I shall never know, but there they were, or, come to think of it, how they managed to get away again. I wish I had that photo now, as in retrospect, the presence of sheep seems so unlikely, but there they were!

The only path to be kept clear was the one to the coal place which we shovelled clear every day, and put down salt and ashes to prevent us slipping when we fetched in the coal. Even Grandma didn't complain about that as the garden path was quite steep and dangerous. In my wellies I ventured along the path to the green-house, and pulling open the door found it dark with the thickness of snow on the glass roof. Everything was quiet, muffled and eerie.

On the bright mornings we made snowmen, or had snowball fights, or started a small snowball beside the road, and rolled it down the hill all the way to school. It grew bigger and bigger and bigger until it was almost as big as as us and we couldn't push it any further. The school milk was delivered most days, and most days it was frozen. Ice patterns appeared on all the windows and sometimes never thawed from one day to the next. Some windows produced pictures of lovely ferns, sea weeds, fairy gardens, and some windows merely became cloudy. I suppose it must have been caused by different textures of glass, or the way the window faced, but they varied considerably.

We had a little dog called Wendy, who was great fun, very affectionate, and who we would usually just let out on her own to attend to the call of nature. Except, of course, when she came into season, when someone had to take her for a walk on the lead, and dodge and deter the patient collie Shep, who sat on our step waiting hopefully. Inevitably she was in season through the very worst of the weather. I walked with her along Underbank Old Road in the intense cold, along the narrow path trodden in the snow, occasionally venturing into the deep virgin snow on either side. Looking up into the dark sky, I marvelled at the brilliance of the stars. I felt the beauty so intensely the picture remains with me to this day.

That must have been a time of great anxiety, and many old folk died of the cold that winter. Rationing was still on, of course, and there was no such thing as central heating. We had one fire, in the house, but although we built it up every night with slack (small coal) in an attempt to keep the place warm and perhaps even for it to be still alive in the morning, it very rarely was, and the painful business of fire lighting in the cold grey dawn had to be faced yet again. Perhaps we were more fortunate than most as Ivy Cottage had very thick walls and had always been kept in good order by Grandad. We had thick curtains to keep out the cold and various small rugs to conquer the the draughts which came under the front door, but the bathroom was icy. Mam's bedroom had a carpet square but mine was mostly linoleum and very cold to the bare feet. At night I always undressed in front of the fire and then dashed upstairs and into bed where Mam had put a stone hot water bottle, 'Jimmy', to keep me warm. This was a bit perilous, it was indeed very hot and would mostly be wrapped in a piece of old blanket. In the morning, it took some willpower to throw off the bedclothes and get out of bed. The snow clad world outside created a strange, cold, white glare in the room. Once I had braved the icy morning I would run to look at each of the windows; which has the best pictures this morning? Was there any snow to cover up the footprints of yesterday? Somehow, I was always a teeny bit disappointed when there had been no new snowfall. The icicles were huge on the Co-op guttering, and we would break off the smaller ones on the way to school and suck them. A good thing Mam never knew that!

It was during that winter that Auntie Phoebe died, followed a week later by Uncle Friend. There was no crematorium in those days and the ground was so frozen that burial was a great problem. The cemetery was at the top of Rotcher, a steep, winding hill. Bleak and windswept at the best of times, in the harsh winter it was truly desolate, and the job of getting the hearse up the hill must have been a problem. Two burials in the space of a week was a severe blow for any family, especially when the deaths were of very elderly loved ones. I liked Uncle Friend, he was kind and jolly and lived up to his name. Auntie Phoebe, I had found intimidating. She was Grandad's sister. The rest of the family felt that Uncle Friend had stayed alive so long only to see her safely sent home first.

CHAPTER SIX

Mam and Dad

My parents were something of a mismatch, and quite early on I became aware that things were not always happy between them. Courting in their day, meant going out together on one evening during the week, and going out or visiting each other's parents on Saturdays and Sundays. Not a lot of contact, not much chance to find out what the person you loved was really like, and what they did with themselves for the rest of the time. Meeting more often was regarded as 'fast' and was not approved of!

My Dad spent a lot of time at the shop, and his social life when work was finished was the pub. Mam was home-loving, creative, very much family-oriented, and certainly never attracted to visiting public houses on an evening for a drink. Few women well-brought up, church-going family people like her would visit pubs in that capacity in those days, and while Dad apparently said she was welcome to go with him, she did not. She would never have felt comfortable in that environment.

Inevitably, Mam and I grew very close, too close, perhaps, just the two of us, but it was a relationship that went very deep and was very happy for many years, until, in fact, I was grown up and finding myself a boy-friend, but that is another story. To return to my childhood.... we moved to Ivy Cottage in, I think, 1946, to look after Grandma, and after her death in 1951, there was no chance to move again.

Figure 6.1
Mum and Dad's wedding, Grandma Wagstaff is on the right, wearing the long, French lace dress, (I played 'dressing-up' in this one!) Dad's sister, Auntie Mabel is on the left, and the bridesmaids are, Sylvia, Joan and Mary. Uncle Frank is on the left of the photograph, and Grandad Wagstaff is on the right

Dad objected strongly to living in Holmfirth. He, in common with the rest of his family, was a 'towny'. I didn't see a lot of him when I was a child. I remember listening to terrible rows when he arrived home late at night, often rather the worse for drink, and on more than one occasion, I went downstairs, unable to keep quiet any longer and verbally attacked him, in defence of Mam. These were dreadful experiences. The force of them comes back to me now, my throat sore and aching with sobs and with shouting, my eyes hot with tears, and the strength of the rage welling up in me uncontrollably. I was powerless to express myself, powerless to change anything, in waters too deep for me to understand.

I remember now the silly gaze, the inability to speak clearly, the smell, the fact that the person I knew had gone away somewhere and I was left with a stranger.

Poor Mam, she so wanted us to be a happy family, to share meals and outings together, and do all the things she remembered from her young days. Dad worked long hours at the shop and then declared he was 'entitled to some pleasure', and went out to the George Hotel or the White Swan, the Conservative Club or the Shoulder of Mutton. He would arrive home on the eleven o'clock bus. Wednesday was his half-day, and he would be home at about three or three-thirty, going out again for the evening at about eight.

Divorce was unthinkable. The stigma, the disgrace, would have affected Mam's every moment and her every social contact. So, as in so very many cases, they stayed together.

In spite of this unhappiness, I still recall some good times with him. Sometimes on a Wednesday, he would bring home a quart of mussels for tea, and we would cook them in the old enamel pan, on the fire. I thought it fascinating. I would help to pull the moss from the shells, which were tightly closed. Then into the pan they would go, and gradually the shells would open, out would spill the sea water and the mussels would be cooked. The smell of the sea would fill the room! We sat to the table and removed the fish from the shells with our fingers, feeling them to make sure there was no grit or seed pearls in them, then dipping them in a saucer of vinegar and pepper, and popping them into our mouths! Delicious! I was never allowed more than two or three and he always insisted that

I ate lots of bread and butter, in case they should 'mussel' me, give me an upset tummy I suppose. Thankfully, they never did.

Dad was a great whistler, and on occasions, when the mood took us, we would whistle together tune after tune, getting steadily more shrill and ear-piercing, and driving Mam to distraction.

At one period, I remember, we went out for walks together on Sunday afternoons around the Valley, and that was most enjoyable. I knew the area well; I had walked the hills and lanes alone for a long time, when Mam was at her wits end what to do with me while she looked after Grandma, and now it was good to share it with Dad.

Walking was a popular pastime in the days before the motor car was universally owned. Often on Sunday afternoons we would set off, Mam, Dad and me, catch the bus to Holmbridge and then walk up to the village of Holme, right at the foot of Holme Moss. Sometimes we took the road up Holme Banks, passed the Holme Silver Band room, and on, up beyond the houses of the watermen, who tended the reservoirs. It was steep and long, and usually hot as we only set out on such an expedition on a fine day. Other times we would walk up the opposite side of the valley, up Brown Hill, and from time to time we could see across to Holme Banks. From this road, I seem to recall, the view was better. We passed Brown Hill Reservoir and always stopped to watch with wonder the overflow, slipping in regular curves down the narrow channel to the river below. Then, across the embankment we went and so to the village of Holme. Very occasionally, we caught the bus to Holme, and walked from there, right to the top of the Moss and back down to the village again, but it was very steep and winding. There we saw the sheep nibbling the tough grass, or sheltering from the wind among the grey rocks. Harebells bloomed by the roadside, fragile and delicate , but amazingly tough when I tried to pluck them. When I succeeded, they died very quickly in the hot squeeze of my hand. Usually on these pleasant and energetic afternoons, we would stop at the pub in Holme, the Golden Fleece. This establishment had a prewar reputation for fine ham and eggs, and even then, being out in the country, would sometimes come up with fresh eggs and a bit of ham! It was a small old fashioned place, with a stone-flagged floor and tables with cast iron legs. It was always cool and dim, in the afternoon when we arrived, the bar closed of course, and the slightly bitter smell of ale which I found agreeable and refreshing.

After the great flood of 1944, when the embankment of Bilberry Reservoir was breached, our expeditions took a different direction as we watched the diggers and earth-moving machinery building the embankment for the new Digley Reservoir, and we would stand at the nearest vantage point and look in bewilderment at the apparent chaos. Gradually, the plan could be seen and order was created, the embankment was finally complete and the dam filled with water. These were happy, contented days, warm with sunshine and love.

My mother was born in Ivy Cottage and apart from the seven or eight years, from her marriage to Grandad's death, lived all her life there. It was part of her, it was home. Her roots were deep into the earth there, no matter how often or how strongly she occasionally wished to move away. This strength of feeling, I inherited. I loved the cottage, the garden, Kippax Row, the view across the valley to Damhouse and up the valley to Choppards and Tinker's Monument and the moors beyond.

It was a good feeling, a good place to be. It was full of history and legend, peopled with strong individuals who took a perverse pride in the steepness of the hills and the depth of the snow!

Mam was a pretty, plump lady, with wide grey eyes and thick dark brown hair. Her plumpness was always a trouble to her and she spent much of her time, or so it seemed to me, looking at and considering various types and styles of corset! Ladies were still laced into whalebone straitjackets in those days, rows of hooks and eyes and yards of laces to thread up and tie, and tuck the knot in somewhere!

She loved music and reading, and in fact ordered for me a set of the works of Charles Dickens, from Foyle's Bookshop in London. They were, of course, second hand, but books were very scarce during the war, and who knew how long such a state of affairs would continue? 'Christine must have them', and I have them still.

Figure 6.2

Mam, shortly before her marriage.

She was very clever with her fingers and knitted and sewed for me and for herself constantly. I still remember some of the clothes she made for me, a twinset in Fair Isle, with four colours, which taxed her rather, and took a very long time. There was a blue knitted dressing gown which lasted me for ages, and was then pulled back and made into a jumper! There is a photograph of me at the age of about six, in a blue skirt and a white satin blouse with short, gathered sleeves. The outfit was completed with a short collarless bolero.

I also remember with rather less pleasure, a bathing costume which she knitted. Wool was hard to come by during the war and often of very poor quality. This was rusty red, and so very rough that it made me quite sore, like having sand in unmentionable places. In the end, I refused to wear it.

She did

Figure 6.3
Christine at about nine years old in the blue skirt and satin blouse Mam made.

100

beautiful embroidery,tablecloths, pillow slips, cushion-covers, and taught me all these skills; we did them together. Later, when I was in my teens, she did a course at night school each winter, and there she learned leather-work and woodwork

Mam and I were so close, so much a part of each other, her presence and memory are a 'feeling' as much as individual memories. We enjoyed each other's company, laughed a lot, did most things together. She took me to Church and taught me a reverence for God and for worship. She introduced me to books, especially the set of Dickens, which she read, and read bits to me, long before I was old enough to read them for myself. She took me on shopping expeditions, picnics, to the theatre and the pantomime. She took me on holiday and included me in everything she did. She found an Elocution teacher for me and opened up a world of wonder and delight that has been a constant joy to me throughout my life. She taught me to cook and sew, and although she was no lover of housework, I was taught to clean, to wash and to iron. I took great pleasure in this, enjoying doing all these tasks with her, and when she went out to work, I enjoyed doing it for her.

Mam had some really lovely china and glass, mostly wedding presents; so beautiful in fact, that they seldom saw the light of day! She also had some lovely table linen, and these fine things came out at Christmas, high days and holidays, and when we had visitors. The rest of the time we used the old odd crockery from the cupboard, some of it belonging to Grandma; mugs and pint pots were easier to wash up than cups and saucers and less likely to be broken. I remember her embarrassment when someone called at teatime and the table was laid with mugs! That never happened again! Sometimes, on a Saturday afternoon, we would get out the fine china and the lace tablecloth and have our tea in grand style, just the two of us.

The radio, 'wireless', was our constant companion. I used to go through the Radio Times each week and underline the pieces of music we particularly enjoyed (concert programmes were always printed in full in those days). There was music from opera, light opera, Ivor Novello, Strauss, Offenbach, Lehar, and at Christmas, Handel's Messiah. We listened to these programmes together, usually sewing or ironing the while. Northern Children's Hour was famous for the quality of its programmes and drama, and between five o'clock and six o'clock every evening we would listen to the wide variety of all that it could offer, from nature programmes to current affairs, quizzes and plays, which I liked best of all: Biggles stories by Capt. W. E. Johns, Bunkle stories by M. Pardoe, 'The Deep Woodlanders' by Elleston Trevor, the Noel Streatfield stories, especially 'Ballet Shoes' and the Jennings stories by Anthony Buckeridge. They were compulsive listening, and incidentally introduced us to other pieces of classical music hitherto unknown to us. I remember the music used for 'Ballet Shoes' was Intermezzo No. 2 from 'The Jewels of the Madonna' by Wolf Ferrari. We enjoyed the music and the lovely long title almost as much! 'Chanson de Matin' by Elgar accompanied the Bunkle stories, delightful! We listened and discussed it all together. Occasionally, they would put on a play with unknown children taking the parts and on one occasion I felt this to be so poorly done that I wrote and said I could do better! I must have been about eleven or twelve at the time. Mam backed me up and I went for an audition, all the way to Manchester. I was unsuccessful, but I was invited to take part in a regional quiz, and Mam took me again to Manchester. It was such a long way - bus to Huddersfield, train to Manchester, and then we had to find our way through the city streets to Piccadilly and Broadcasting House. I reckon Mam was a hero to do it for me; the expense, the time off school for me, a day's work missed for her, virtually a whole day's expedition. Cities did not feature in our daily experience, and Manchester was so big, so busy, so much traffic, so many people jostling and hurrying along the streets. When we finally arrived, we were fed on bread and jam and tea, and then taken to the studio. The Northern team was me and a boy. I can't say that I covered myself with glory, but I survived. I was especially put out because one question was 'What colour is indigo?' Now I well knew that good navy cloth was dyed with indigo, so I said 'blue', but they wanted 'purple'. I think my indignation carried me on and quite took away any sadness that we hadn't won! I was presented with a book token which I later used to buy myself a good dictionary.

Mam was game for almost anything, from picnics on the moors, picking bilberries and blackberries, to an expedition to the theatre or pantomime, joining the local Dramatic Society, or taking me on holiday at a time when many beaches were still being cleared after the War. Her influence on me was all enveloping, her sayings, her beliefs, her attitude to life and the way she simply got on with the job of looking after her mother and trying at the same time to keep a rocky marriage afloat. I admire her enormously. She was a great one for proverbs and sayings and wise words, and had a quote for almost every occasion, and sometimes more than one! 'Early to bed and early to rise, makes a man healthy, wealthy and wise'. How many times have I heard that?! Grandma's favourite was, *'An hour before midnight is worth two after'*!

Thrift, a quality which was, and still is, highly prized in Holmfirth, became during the war and the years that followed, an essential part of life and keeping a family fed and clothed. The old maxims were in frequent use. 'Make do and mend', and 'Take care of the pence and the pounds will take care of themselves', this at a time when a pound, twenty shillings, was a great deal of money. There were also scathing comments for people who didn't consider *the value of their purchases and didn't buy good quality 'Penny wise and pound foolish'* was quoted then, or *'A fool and his money are soon parted'*. When the money would not stretch to luxuries of any kind, the stern words of wisdom were *'to cut your coat according to your cloth'*. Mam had only a passing acquaintance with Shakespeare, but *'neither a borrower nor a lender be'* was a philosophy shared with Hamlet! A good old Yorkshire word in frequent use was 'thoil', which meant that some object was over-priced, and although one had the money and could really afford it, it was not considered good value. 'I can't thoil it' she would say. Money, perforce, had to be greatly respected, it being in such short supply, and another wry comment of hers was that *'Money was made round to go round, but it goes round some people more than others'*. No one enjoyed living like this, and the dire warning was given to yound people anxious to wed, *'When poverty comes in the door, love flies out through the window.'*

The small thrifty economies of life were much in evidence during the time of rationing. Hard times in the Textile trade had prepared the West Riding people well. Experience is a great teacher. A freshly baked loaf must never be cut the same day. If it was left until the morrow it would slice much more easily.

104

The jam jar would be scraped out so thoroughly that you could hardly tell what colour the jam had been, and an extra slice of bread had been made sweet and tasty! If a parcel arrived, the brown paper was removed very carefully, and lovingly folded and put away for future use. The knotted string would be meticulously untied and wound into a ball. A freshly baked loaf must never be cut the same day. If it was left until the morrow it would slice much more easily. The jam jar would be scraped out so thoroughly that you could hardly tell what colour the jam had been, and an extra slice of bread had been made sweet and tasty! If a parcel arrived, the brown paper was removed very carefully, and lovingly folded and put away for future use. The knotted string would be meticulously untied and wound into a ball. The last slither of soap would be stuck to the new tablet, and thoroughly worn out underwear was used for dishcloths, floor cloths and dusters. The thought of actually buying such a thing was anathema to Mam, as it was to many others.

Even now I still feel guilty at buying dishcloths and dusters, and old underwear still provides us with floor cloths! Many a small child's dress or pair of trousers was made from an adult sized garment that no longer fitted, or was showing signs of wear; jumpers and cardigans were unravelled and the wool washed. Some were dyed before being knitted up into another garment.

She had a strong Christian faith, although she was not an exceptionally regular churchgoer. One service on Sunday was enough, none of the two or three meetings of Chapel folk

I was confirmed when I was about thirteen years old, when the Bishop of Wakefield visited Holmfirth for the ceremony. Several of us were confirmed that day, from various churches in the area. It was considered to be a great privilege for the occasion to happen in our own parish church. I borrowed a white dress for the event from my school friend June, funds, as ever, not running to the extravagance of a garment which would only be worn once. The service was held on a Sunday afternoon, and I can remember very little of it, only the part when the Bishop went up into the pulpit, placed his purple velvet hat on the edge near the reading desk, and it almost slipped off! He just stopped its fall in time!

Figure 6.4
'Mam'

106

Hopes had run high that Dad would come to Church for the occasion, but the nearest he got was to walk down Underbank to meet us on our way home.

After I was confirmed, she and I would often go together to the seven o'clock or eight o'clock Communion on Sunday mornings. I have to admit it was more likely to be the eight o'clock service, but even so, the Church in the early morning was beautiful, just a few people gathered in the quiet. It was almost worth dragging yourself out of a warm bed just for the walk down Underbank in the cold bright air, but the service made it doubly good. It set a sound, good note for the day.

Mam had an open disposition and lived her life by a set of strong people, and tender to a degree. I cannot imagine her engaging in anything underhand, or dealing in untruths or lies. She was no 'wheeler dealer' and the black market in forbidden goodies passed us by. She was not totally naïve, however, and she made a point of saying, *'Handsome is as handsome does'*, and *'Fine feathers don't make fine birds'*. In other words, don't be deceived by good looks and finery. She did, however, have one saying which gives pause for thought, *'Blind a good husband in one eye, bad one in both'*. She had learned to survive! *'Pride goeth before a fall'* is still a well-known proverb. Less well known are Mam's words, *'Pride must abide'*, especially spoken to me (and to herself) when new fine shoes pinched, when earrings nipped and when waistbands , or corsets, were uncomfortably tight.

When I was about ten, I was given an autograph book, and the first entry, on the first page was from Mam.

Your future lies before you,

Like a sheet of driven snow.
Be careful how you tread,
For every mark will show'

She knew me, knew my strong will and my strong temper. She so much wanted me to be a good person, but this closeness could not continue, for as she and Dad became further estranged from one another, she came to rely on me and my company more than ever. And gradually, in my late teens, I felt the need for my freedom and my independence.

CHAPTER SEVEN

The Seasons.

The year was shaped by the Church Festivals, Christmas, Easter, Whitsuntide, and Chapel Anniversaries. Each brought its own treats, special food, families and friends to visit, and considerable preparations beforehand, especially cleaning and polishing floors and furniture, baking cakes and perhaps cooking a piece of ham or ox tongue. Quite often, the produce from the garden would have its first harvesting, in particular, Grandad's tomatoes which were first picked every year for Underbank Chapel Anniversary Weekend. The fact that we were not chapel-goers did not prevent us celebrating their anniversary!

Winters in the Pennines were long and cold and wet, and always there was snow. The first signs of spring were eagerly watched for, the first catkins, the first little blue scillas beside the front door, the evenings getting just a little bit lighter and the sun just a little bit warmer.

Shrove Tuesday, Pancake Day, was always fun. I loved pancakes and the house would gather a faint blue haze as Mam fried them on the stove and we ate them, speckled and hot, straight from the pan, with sugar and lemon or orange juice squeezed onto them. They were mouth-wateringly good, pancakes have never tasted so good since then!

Mothering Sunday quickly followed and I remember being told about the young girls who has been sent away from home into service, and how they were allowed to visit their mothers on Mid-Lent Sunday; hence the name Mothering Sunday, or so I thought. They would walk back home along the lanes carrying a basket in which they had the gift of Simnel Cake for her, and would pick the violets from the hedgerows along the way. I was charmed, being a romantic little soul, and resolved that my mother would always have the traditional bunch of violets for Mothering Sunday. I had no awareness of the loneliness the girls must have felt, being separated from their loved ones, of the long hours and hard work with little time off; the realization of all that came much later. All I saw was the pretty picture of girls in long dresses and white mob caps, walking through the spring countryside on a day that was special and when the sun always shone. As violets do not grow wild around Holmfirth my resolution caused me some problems, and I used to save my pocket money and buy them from the nursery. It always had to be a secret, a surprise for Mam on the Sunday morning, and I would sneak them into the house and hide them under the bed in Grandad's old tin trunk. I would produce them at breakfast time, when Mam was beginning to think I had forgotten, and she was always delighted, and wore them pinned to her coat for the special afternoon service at Church.

Palm Sunday was the next red letter day for me. We children used to gather twigs of pussy willow, which we called 'palm', and put them in a vase and watch the soft grey furry buds open, and sometimes become freckled with golden pollen.

I loved Lent and Easter at church. All through Lent there would be the plain purple altar cloth, no flowers, and it was all very solemn. And then, Easter morning, the altar decked in the lovely white and gold embroidered cloths,

110

with beautiful white lilies in the two silver vases. When you went into Church on Easter Day, you knew it was wonderful, triumphant and glorious! The Easter hymn rang out,

'Christ the Lord is risen today,
Alleluia'.

Every year it brought tears to my eyes and a lump to my throat; it still does! I have always been moved by the story of Holy Week, Good Friday and Christ's Resurrection, and each year, even now, I plan to read the whole story again, and sadly, I rarely manage it. I was given, at Sunday school, a small green paper-backed copy of St. Luke's Gospel, and I read it avidly from cover to cover. I think even after all these years St. Luke is my favourite gospel.

Easter in Holmfirth was celebrated in a very practical way. Because of the difficulties with the mill machinery, so I was given to understand, Good Friday was never a holiday. Church was open all day with prayers and solemn music, but the looms clattered as always. Instead, the holiday was Easter Monday and Easter Tuesday, back to work on the Wednesday. Maybe we were just Philistines, but work had to be done, cloth had to be woven and jobs and livelihoods had to be protected.

Easter was the first holiday of the year, but the first holiday when you could reasonably expect to have good weather was Whitsuntide, and in those days it was a holiday from work. Since Spring Bank Holiday was invented, Whitsuntide has rather got lost and overlooked by the general population, which seems a great shame to me. I remember the Vicar telling us that Whitsuntide was the most important of all the Christian festivals.

As the days grew warmer, the countryside and the gardens blossomed. At Ivy Cottage we had a most beautiful white lilac tree which was usually in flower for the festival, and the scent was heady and delicious. The laburnum tree had long, long drooping clusters of yellow flowers, followed by small 'pea pods' of seeds which I was regularly warned about as they are very poisonous. I found this strange, such a beautiful tree to have such deadly seeds. The cherry tree, too, would be in flower, and the scent of the newly cut lawns and the chance to play on the grass delighted my senses more as each year passed. Across our small valley, Swan Wood was full of bluebells and the pale green fronds of bracken were just breaking through the misty blue carpet. We could hear the cuckoo calling. It was the very essence of early summer days.

The build-up to Whitsuntide was long and exciting. Two weeks before the holiday, was the Annual Band Contest, and on that Saturday, the Civic Hall rang to the strains of music and the town was filled with bandsmen (always men in those days) in their splendid uniforms. There were many bands in the Holme Valley and the surrounding area and competition was keen. The adjudicators sat in a small enclosed box of a place in the centre of the hall and were only able to identify the bands by the number, drawn just at the commencement - so there could be no possible favouritism. Many were the tales of bands arranging secret signals so that they could be identified! The public houses did very well on that day, too, it being the custom for a band to hire a room in which to have a last practice. This was very convenient,as blowing hard created quite a thirst, and it was not unknown for some bandsmen to be slightly merry before they mounted the platform. The appeal of Band Contest Saturday grew greater as I grew older and more able to appreciate the music, and the musicians!

The following week was known as Holmfirth Feast, when the fair arrived in town, and there were dodgems, big wheel and roundabouts. I can still remember how I hated it, the noise, the smell and the speed of it all. I also remember, or is it just that it was spoken of so often, my Grandad walking down to Holmfirth to meet me and Mam, in the days when we went to Ivy Cottage each weekend and Dad was in the RAF. He had come to meet us 'to take t'child to t'feast!' Sadly, the child did not want to go to the Feast! I must have been persuaded to go at least once as I can recall riding on the 'Cocks and Horses', sedately going up and down and round and round, and clinging on to the pole for dear life.

It was on Feast Sunday that the park came into its own. Little frequented during the rest of the year, for the Feast and for Whitsun, a tiered platform was built and the local chapel choirs would fill the platform, and their congregations, friends and neighbours and everyone would flock to the park for a grand 'Sing'. There were pieces sung by the massed choirs and much enthusiastic congregational hymn singing.

Whitsuntide meant new clothes, and many expeditions were made to Huddersfield to buy them, with a great deal of discussion and trying on and perhaps turning up the hem to be sure it would fit for a long time. Mam made dresses for me very often, but the Whitsuntide dress had to be special, and hopes were always high that the weather would be warm enough to go without a coat, and be able to show it off.

Sometimes, Mam took me to Leeds for my clothes,

and that was a very long and exciting, not to say exhaust-ing, trip. First the walk to Holmfirth, then the six mile bus journey to Huddersfield, a walk to the other end of the town and finally, a forty-five minute bus journey to Leeds. We had our dinner in a café, wicker chairs and glass-topped tables, so wonderfully elegant, but the traffic was terrifying to me, used only to a very rural existence. In addition to buses, cars and lorries, there were trams!

Figure 7.1
An example of the Leeds trams which terrified me as a child.
You can just see the lines, and the overhead wires in
the photograph.

They were monsters of the road, running on iron tracks, and with a kind of pole from the roof of the tram to the overhead wire. They were tall and narrow, and they swayed and clanged, and made a metallic grinding noise as they passed. Perhaps the most frightening thing of all was that they were the same at both ends, so I couldn't tell if it would come towards us or move away! Crossing Briggate, clutching Mam's hand, was a daunting experience, no zebra crossings in those days. Later on, I actually travelled on a tram and was intrigued to see that the backs of the seats could be swung from forwards to back so that whichever way the tram was going, the passengers could face the front in comfort. The steering wheel, there was one at each end, had a knob on it, and the driver stood at his post.

All this excitement for the new clothes! When I was quite small, a straw bonnet with tiny flowers, and ribbons to tie under my chin was a must, very pretty, and only worn on Sundays for Church. Later on, the bonnet gave way to a hat, a mushroom hat, we girls called it, felt, with a brim, and this again was only worn on special occasions and Sundays. A new coat and dress, shoes and gloves would complete the outfit, although one year I remember having an umbrella, too, with a smooth handle and pale pink flowers on it. I spent a whole summer wishing it would rain so I could put it up and actually use it! Only on Sundays, of course!

I suffered for vanity even as a child. I remember vividly a pair of pale blue ankle-strap shoes. I had pestered Mam and wanted them for so long, that she finally gave in and bought them for me. They pinched a bit when I tried them on in the shop, but they were so pretty I never admitted it. Within a matter of weeks, they pinched so much I couldn't wear them at all. Mam was so cross with me. She gave them away to a little girl, a member of one of the big families of the village, and was really vexed to see the child playing hopscotch in them, the shoes by then being almost unrecognisable, they were so scuffed. 'I'll never give them anything again. They were so expensive, and look at them now!'

Whit Sunday was important with the Church Service after Sunday school. Families visited each other for Tea, in their new clothes, of course, a proper 'High Tea' with ham and tongue and stand pie, pickles and salad, fruit trifle and two or three kinds of cake. How this was managed when rationing was in force, I really don't know. I can only say that I remember these occasions as feasts.

Whit Monday was even more of an event. It was the era of Whit Walks, and all, or nearly all the Churches and Chapels in Holmfirth would muster all their Sunday school 'scholars' and have a walk of witness around the district, from their own church to Victoria Park in the centre of the town. There the scholars would mount the platform for a Sing. The many silver prize bands in the area had a great day, a day of glory with their splendid uniforms and shining instruments, and especially if one of the local bands had won in the recent Band Contest! Each church would hire a band to lead their procession; the banner would be taken down from the wall where it had hung all the rest of the year. Two of the teachers or perhaps older teenage boys, would carry it, and several of the younger boys would be proud to hold the tasselled ropes. The banners were beautiful; some had a picture of a lamb, some a picture of Jesus the Good Shepherd with lamb and crook; often they were blue with a gold fringe, and some had pictures in rich colours, crimson, green and gold. On a windy day it must have been hard work to carry them, definitely not a task for the weak! There were stopping places along the route where everyone would gather round, people came out of their houses to join in, and hymns were sung from a special sheet. It was a joy to sing in the open air with the band, and some of the hymns came from the chapels and were quite unfamiliar, but had good tunes and, to me, a different imagery to our rather restrained 'Hymns Ancient and Modern'. I particularly remember the words '*to rid my soul of one dark blot*', which impressed me. Fascinating! More people joined the procession at each stopping place and the crowd grew greater as the park was reached. Who would be first there, Holmfirth Wesley, or Lane Congregational? Where is the contingent from St. Johns? Then the strains of the band would be heard and we knew they were well on their way.

There was always a bustle in our house to get dinner over and the dishes washed in good time. I was ready, in my new finery, and waited at the front gate to hear the first strains of music. If the sky was grey, would it rain and spoil everything, or would it hold off until we were all in the park, and then pour down? However, the sky cleared a little, coats were definitely to be worn and the tales of Whit Mondays that were so hot the 'gas tar' melted in the road, made me, at any rate, wish everyone who remembered those days would shut up! Sometimes it was sunny, of course, but it always seemed to be necessary to wear my new coat. The shoes always pinched by the time I had walked in the procession, and my feet ached, but vanity always prevailed!

After the Sing in the Park, each Sunday School went back to their own schoolroom for a Grand Tea. I can see and smell the tall tea urns as I write, and each child received a 'school cake' to take home. This was a sweetened dough bun with fruit and candied peel, and a sticky top. The day concluded with a Gala in the evening with races and prizes.

The Parish Church, which we attended, had discontinued its Whit Monday celebrations. Strange when I remember Mr Dangerfield, the vicar, telling us that Whitsuntide was the most important of the Christian festivals. So I joined in with another Sun-day school. Sometimes I walked with Underbank Chapel who were Methodists, and sometimes with Holmfirth Wesleyan Chapel, Methodists, too, I suppose, but the old name lingered. I think Underbank Chapel has to have been the best. To hear the sound of the band coming up Underbank Old Road, and see the banner over the tops of the walls, almost toppling over the hill was so steep and narrow, made my heart pound in my chest with emotion and excitement, and brought a lump to my throat, so that I feared I would disgrace myself and cry! The tears were always near when we sang the hymns, and even now, after many years in The Salvation Army, the sight and sound of a band on the march affects me in much the same way.

Most Whit Mondays in my memory merge and I cannot distinguish one from another. One, however, does stand out. I was five years old, almost six, the year being 1944. Being so young I did not join in the Walks, in fact we still lived in Lockwood and only visited Ivy Cottage at weekends and holidays, so I had no links with any Sunday school. On this occasion, I walked down to the park with Mam. I remember my dress clearly; it was pale blue, with tiny, fine stripes, or perhaps the material was woven into fine ribs. At all events, it was new and pretty and I loved it. The afternoon was very hot and became rather overcast and oppressive. Walking back up Underbank was a long toil and we were hot and sticky. Grandma and Grandad had prepared tea, the table was laid and all was ready when we arrived home. As Grandma was putting on the kettle, the first roll of thunder was heard, rumbling and echoing among the hills, and the sky rapidly darkened. Now, Grandma always made a great drama out of a thunder storm and so it was that day. The mirrors had to be covered, so that the lightning should not get trapped in the house; the door must be open wide so that if a thunderbolt should come down the chimney, it could go out by the door! No one was allowed to pick up a knife, far too dangerous, the steel would attract the lightning and strike you dead! So there we were, doors open, mirrors covered and no one allowed to eat Tea because of the knives! The storm continued for a very long time, the sheet lightning became the more dangerous forked lightening, and no rain fell. The weather had been dry and sunny for several weeks and the fear of fire was predominant. The tension grew as the storm continued, the thunder cracked and rolled heavily. The noise was frightening, and we tried to count between the flash of lightning and the noise of the thunder to see how far away the heart of the storm really was. The heart of the storm was right overhead and still no rain fell. For me, sitting on the small leather settee with the smooth brown velvet cushions, it seemed an age, and when at last, the first splashes of rain fell, it was a great relief. The rain fell like arrows, thick, heavy and fierce. There was much jolly talk of people moving furniture around upstairs, presumably to reassure me and make the whole experience light-hearted. I felt safe enough, I don't remember being seriously afraid, but I did want my tea!

Eventually, of course, the storm subsided and the ferocity of the rain diminished. We had tea, and I went to bed, and that was the end of another exciting day for me. The storm had wreaked terrible damage in Holmfirth; Bilberry Reservoir had breached its embankment in the cloudburst, and the flood waters had poured down the Holme Valley, sweeping away walls and houses, shops, trees and hedges. The bridges in Holmfirth were gone and the devastation was incalculable. Three people lost their lives that day. I only learned many years later that German prisoners of war who were housed in the area, helped with the rescue operation. There was little publicity about the disaster because the Normandy Landings, D Day, was planned for the following week, and details of weather conditions anywhere in Britain were strictly censored.

This was the third Holmfirth flood. In 1777 and again in 1852, similar disasters had occurred.

Figure 7.2
Holmfirth Flood, May 29th, 1944

The moors above the town have many reservoirs and the Holme Valley is very susceptible. Thankfully, our little tributary, the Ribble, was quite safe. Tales were told in the days that followed of how all the rats in the basements of houses on Hollowgate, beside the river, and in the mills down the valley, had all vacated the premises and had moved out to higher ground, uncannily aware of the impending disaster.

My own recollection of the damage is of being taken the following week along the road to Holmbridge, and there was a huge 'bite' out of the road, an enormous semi-circle where the waters had surged and bitten away the whole road, leaving only the further pavement against the hillside. The villages of Holme, Holmbridge and Hinchcliffe Mill were cut off for some time.

Figure 7.3
Digley.
The reservoir was built after the Flood.

Of course, re-building took place, the bridges were re-built and a stone inscribed with the height of the flood-waters, unbelievably as far as I can recall, about eight feet from the level of the bridge! A new reservoir was built, and many pleasant Sunday afternoons were spent visiting the site to see how it progressed and to marvel at the sheer enormity of the project, and how order began to grow out of the chaos.

As the summer progressed, holidays and trips to the seaside were planned and discussed at length, and longed for. Chapel Anniversaries provided the next local excitement. Underbank Chapel was always a lively place and in common with others in the area, the choir tackled the classical repertoire with enthusiasm. Haydn's 'Creation', 'Olivet to Calvary' for Easter, maybe Handel's 'Messiah' and a pantomime at Christmas; teas and celebrations for the older people and outings for the children were all part of their activities. With such an energetic and committed congregation, their anniversary was a big event - more visitors, more family celebrations! A tiered platform was erected on Dover Lane for the choir and the Sunday school scholars, and a band would be hired for a good traditional 'Sing'. Mam used to be full of admiration for their activities when things at Church were rather restrained to say the least!

Harvest Festival was rather good at Church. The building was always decorated with fresh produce from all the local gardeners, who brought their flowers, and apples, pears, plums, cabbages, cauliflowers, leeks and tomatoes, and always a sheaf of corn. There was always a bunch of luscious black grapes hanging from the lectern, looked at longingly by all of us children. No one ever had grapes unless they were very ill indeed!

After Harvest, the nights began to draw in, and gardens were given a good tidying up ready for winter. All Grandad's chrysanthemums which had stood in rows in their pots, were moved into the greenhouse when the tomatoes finished, and the scent of their blooms was sweet and pungent and very autumnal. He was very proud of them, raising them from cuttings every year. It always fascinated me when Grandad used to go along the rows of pots, tapping them with a small special stick, and by this method was able to tell if they needed watering!

The fresh chill of autumn breezes would send all the mothers to seek out the woollies, the coats and the scarves. Excitement would mount as the posters advertising Standard Fireworks appeared in the shop windows, and Bonfire Night approached. By the time we moved to Ivy Cottage the war was over and the blackout was banished to history, so bonfires were built with great enthusiasm. Wood was collected from gardens and stacked in several places up and down the Valley where people gathered to join in the fun.

At home we always had a bonfire in the garden, getting rid of all the rubbish before winter came. Somehow, we always had a few fireworks although money was always short. One year, when the great day fell on a Wednesday, Dad came home with a ten shilling box! This was unheard of extravagance. There were lots of 'Thunder Flashes' and 'Jumping Jacks' which I didn't enjoy much, but the 'Roman Candles' and 'Catherine Wheels', 'Snowstorms' and 'Volcanoes' were wonderful. And 'Sparklers', I loved 'Sparklers', bravely holding them at arm's length in a gloved hand.

Mam always had a supply of treacle toffee to suck against the cold wind and the smoke. The smell of burning leaves and wood smoke and the sheer delight of poking the fire with a long stick and dodge the eddies of smoke blowing the flames in all directions was exciting, and then there was the ritual of standing the fireworks on a flat stone and lighting the blue touch paper with a glowing strand of 'touch'. This was a thick piece of soft cord or wick which smouldered aromatically, and slowly burnt away as the evening went on. The rockets were always a bit of a disappointment though. There was all the buildup, balancing the rocket on its stick in a milk bottle, making sure it was facing away from us all, lighting the blue touch paper and retiring to a safe place. Then it smouldered, and we waited. Had it gone out? Did we dare to go back and light it again....and then, up it went! That was it. No stars, no colours, just a trace of orange sparks and it was over! What a letdown, what an anti-climax.

When the fire had burned low, we went indoors with rosy cheeks and cold hands and a distinctly smoky smell about the hair and the coat and the scarf. Supper was a baked potato eaten piping hot, with butter (or margarine) and salt, squares of homemade   Parkin, this was a cake made for the occasion, with oatmeal, ginger and golden syrup.

First thing the following morning I would go down the garden to examine the ashes of the fire, now damp and lifeless, but very occasionally still warm if the night had been fine. There was the milk bottle that had held the rocket, the charred remains of the Catherine Wheel still attached by its pin to the shed door, the empty shells of the 'Snowstorm' and the 'Golden Rain'. The smell of smoke still lingered in the morning air as I went to school to exchange stories of the great night with everyone else. It always seems a shame to me that children can no longer enjoy a good bonfire and 'squibs' in the garden. I always made sure that my own boys enjoyed the fun safely. Stuart in particular enjoyed himself, dancing around the fire, poking it energetically, and throwing potatoes into the heart of the flames, to rake them out later, black and smooth as pebbles and totally delicious. Nowadays the custom seems to be huge bonfires with firework displays; bigger, better, safer, with less involvement and trouble. Being realistic, many children suffered burns, and hospitals were always reported to be busy on the fifth of November, so it has to be good that there are fewer accidents. For myself, I can never remember hearing of any of my school friends or acquaintances getting hurt, and I still have a tinge of regret for the passing of a homely celebration that I enjoyed.

With Bonfire Night over, the days grew still shorter, the mornings dark and raw, making it hard to get out of bed, no central heating, no fire when Mam was working and left home on the seven o'clock bus.

We must have been hardy souls, feet on to the bare lino, a quick wash in cold water! The frosty patterns on the windows were wonderful and I would run to examine and compare them. Sometimes, at the end of November or the early days of December, we would have snow and that was really exciting. Perhaps it would last until Christmas! It never did. Occasionally we did have snow for the big day and that was wonderful. Sometimes it was just a very keen frost, and that was almost as good, but when it was just another cold day, a 'green Christmas', that was a real anti-climax for me and it didn't feel like Christmas at all! In fact, I confess that feeling still prevails with winters growing milder with each year that passes. My boys were very dismayed when we moved to the South West and we informed them that snow was quite rare in Paignton.

'Let's go back, then,' they said! Our last Christmas

in Yorkshire was snowy and we were able to enjoy that together.

Christmas was always spent at Ivy Cottage, even before we left our house in Huddersfield and moved in with Grandma. Looking out at the sky on Christmas Eve, when Mam thought I was snugly tucked up in my bed, I would see one very bright star over the dark silhouette of the hill across the valley, which always in my mind was the Christmas Star. Still is, I look for it even today! There were a few small lights from the half-dozen or so cottages at Damhouse, and everything else was in darkness. I would look for Father Christmas, and listen for sleigh bells long after I should have been asleep.

One Christmas, I had to sleep in Grandma's big double bed, with the high black rails at head and foot; a bed upon which you laid rather than snuggled into. It was hard and unyielding, rather, I felt at the time, like Grandma!

From where I lay, I could see the landing light shining through the crack of the just-open door, and hear the faint voices from downstairs, the wireless, the creaks of the old house; I could smell the clean linen under my head, cool with lavender, and the scent of polish.

The first sounds on Christmas morning were, quite often, the strains of 'Christians Awake' and 'Hark the Herald Angels Sing,' played by a small group of bandsmen from Hade Edge Band. That was wonderful, the day was marked as special, and Dad would open the front door to hear the music better, and 'to let Christmas in'.

The custom was to leave a pillow slip hanging beside the fire place, and sometimes a glass of milk and a mince pie for Father Christmas. The threat was that if I was a naughty girl I would get no presents, instead,

Father Christmas would leave a sack of cinders! On more than one occasion I can remember being quite worried! I suppose the build up to Christmas was quite exciting even in those wartime days.

Presents were often homemade, although that was never apparent to me at the time. I remember one year finding a splendid doll's house beside my pillow case, and remarking that it wouldn't fit in, and then in my excitement, desperately tugging at the roof to open it and look inside. Mam gently restrained me and showed me how the front of the house had a catch and the whole opened like a door, to show upstairs and downstairs; just two rooms, with all the furniture. Grandad had made and painted the whole thing, and Mam had made the pillows, cushions, counterpanes and everything. It was beautiful. Years later, I gave it away to a children's home. I hope the children enjoyed it as much as me. I wish I had it now.

Another present made by my Grandad was a little sewing box. It was dark oak with pretty beading on the lid, and pink cushioning inside, for pins and things. It was lined with pink and had a little tray which lifted out. I still have it, although after years of use the hinges came off the lid and have never been replaced.

There must have been hours of patience and love put into these gifts. They brought me hours of pleasure.

We never had a real Christmas tree, due, I suppose to the war, but we did have a small artificial one, given to me by Uncle Vic and Auntie Elsie. Their daughter, my cousin Sylvia, was by that time grown up. It stood in a little square box, and all the branches folded up to the trunk for storage. They were made of wire with what appeared to be green feathers twisted around them, looking quite effective. The baubles also came from Sylvia; they were very fragile blown glass. There were two tiny trumpets, I remember, which would actually make a sound if you blew them very gently! Several of these delicate ornaments survive to this day, a fish, a clown's face and a lamp. They come out every year, becoming more precious to me as each Christmas passes. Now, my grandson helps me to decorate our tree, a real tree, each year, and he too looks for the old special decorations.

Food is always an important part of Christmas. A turkey would have been too big for us, even if one were available at a price that could be afforded. Usually we had a chicken from a man in Underbank who kept a few hens. Sometimes Dad brought a bird from one of his friends inhe trade, maybe a duck or a guinea fowl, but that was very special indeed!

Mam always made the 'seasoning' herself, what we now refer to as stuffing, although I never remember it being inside the bird. It was always served in a dish separately. I used to help and I hated making the breadcrumbs, scratching my nails against the grater, and it all crumbling in big lumps which all had to be reduced to the right consistency! The end result, however, was well worth the suffering!

Christmas cake, pudding and mince pies were all essential for the feast, then as now. Mam was an excellent cook and no memory is sweeter than that of baking all these good things together with her, with the wireless on, listening to the 'Messiah' or a Carol Concert, and singing along with the music. There was no separate kitchen at Ivy Cottage, and the whole of the living room would be taken up with the activity. It was great fun; the smells were gorgeous, cleaning out the bowl delicious, and the final results, mouth-watering. She must have saved up her ration coupons for many weeks to enable her to make the festive food. As always, the quality of thrift was much prized, and certainly brought its rewards.

Christmas carols must surely be the most evocative music of the whole year. Apart from the essentials , 'While Shepherds'' and 'Hark the Herald', Mam's favourite was 'Silent Night'. Certain carols we were not allowed to sing until Christmas morning, 'Christians Awake' being one, and the last verse of 'O Come all ye Faithful'. For some reason I could never understand, we never sang 'O Little Town of Bethlehem'. Perhaps it was just that our Sunday school teacher, Miss. Shore, just did not like it! We sang it at school, of course, and I love it, especially when when sung to the 'other tune', which I now know is called 'Christmas Carol' in the Salvation Army carol book.

There was no shortage of music for the festive season. The West Riding of Yorkshire is famous for its music making, with the local brass bands, Chapel choirs and the renowned Huddersfield Choral Society, referred to locally as 'the Choral', which was, and still is, internationally acclaimed. Our small village of Underbank was known for a particular tune to 'While Shepherds'. It was an elaborate affair, with many runs and repeats, and was sung best by a group of men whose voices had been gently lubricated with good ale, and were consequently slightly merry. Or so my Mam said!

I have very few memories of any Nativity Play, either at school or at Church. Perhaps the war had something to do with it, but I do remember just one which was presented in Church. Mary was played by one of the old er teenagers, Nora Berry, and the angel, who had to sing, was played by another older teenager, Mary Wagstaff. (Mam always felt she sang off-key) and Christine Shore

Christine Moorhouse and I (always lots of Christines) had to stand near the manger and sing 'Away in a Manger'. I remember clearly having to wear my red dress, which I hated, and I also remember the panic and the humiliation when we more or less fizzled out in the third verse because we weren't sure of the words, and I did want so very much to be Mary or an Angel, or even a King!

We always had a party, War or no! I recall them vividly, all rolled into one; the jelly, the games, and shivering into my party dress, and the shame when I was never 'chosen' in the various ring games, such as: King William was King David's Son, or, All the Royal Races Run'.

I did win a prize, just once, in 'Pass the Parcel'. It was a box, not a tube, of Rowntree's Fruit Pastilles. We always had Santa Claus, too, my Uncle Friend dressed in red and with a grotesque mask to prevent me, or anyone else, recognizing him.

Sometimes, I was taken to the pantomime. The Mother's Union or their Young Wives Group would organize a trip to Leeds or Bradford, to a 'big' one, - as compared to the local Chapel's production; there would be much talk about how well it was presented, the quality and grandeur of the costumes, and how good the transformation scene was. I thought it absolutely magical. When you compare it with the amazing special effects in the theatre today, it was pretty tame, but we knew no different. The magic worked for us. One year, we went see 'Dick Whittington' and the cat walked all around the edge of the Dress Circle in the interval. We were thrilled, until he spoilt the whole effect by removing the head of his costume for the finale! The excitement was tremendous; the anticipation; the gilded grandeur of the theatre, the red plush tip-up seats. To this day, a tangerine, reminds me of these excursions.

The religious meaning of Christmas, and my blossoming Christian faith, is the overriding element of my memories. After I was confirmed, Mam and I would go to Midnight Communion together on Christmas Eve. It was so beautiful, so peaceful! The warm bright church, and lots of people there. It often took half an hour, or longer, for everyone to receive communion, and the whole atmosphere was so full of warmth and good will. The old carols brought the whole story to life, the message of peace and goodwill was true and eternal. We felt it so, in our bones. These were precious moments which influence my life still. The service ended with the singing of 'O Come all yeFaithful', and of course, that was exactly the right time for the last verse,

'Yea, Lord, we greet thee, Born this happy morning'.

It was all over at about a quarter to one. Everyone would wish their friends and neighbours a Happy Christmas, and Mam and I would walk back home to Ivy Cottage. Sometimes we were in time to hear the Underbank Chapel choir setting out on their Carol Singing around the village. They always started by singing 'Hail, Smiling Morn' outside the Chapel. If we heard that, the season was really crowned with joy! The sound of their singing would drift to us from time to time as we fell asleep.

Many years later, Christmas was spent singing and playing carols with my husband, and with my two sons, who were in the Young People's Band at The Salvation Army. We went out to play and sing to various elderly people, sometimes outside their home, under a street lamp, warmly wrapped up in our coats and scarves, with the non-players such as me holding torches, so the children could see their music. Sometimes we went into their tiny living-room, all squashed together, lots of music, lots of laughter, and afterwards, mince pies and chocolate biscuits. On the way home from school, in the car, we would sing carols together, and we knew lots! Good King Wenceslas was good, one of us singing the king and one of us singing the page. It was excellent fun, and more happy, precious memories! We always had a Nativity Play in our Carol Service, and I have written more scripts for this celebration than I can remember! To this day, the old carols telling the story of Jesus' birth are enormously important to me; and the hush and quiet very late on Christmas Eve , the hush one finds with a new born baby; the wonder and the reverence; these things are Christmas to me, all from the influence and love of my mother.

CHAPTER EIGHT

A Woman's Place

'A woman's place is in the home', was a philosophy much in evidence in my childhood, to the extent that when I passed the exam to go to the grammar school, Mam was quite upset to have the comment 'You'll never let her go, will you? She's only a girl; it'll be no good to her'. She was so indignant! She, bless her, had other ideas.

This attitude was perhaps surprising after all the upheaval of the war which was so recently over, when women had to keep the mills, the factories, the shops and offices going, and play their part in the armed services. I suppose the hope was that society would return to pre-war standards and values and the status quo be re-established. I still love the idea of being home with my children and being totally involved in home making and parenthood. Work outside the home could come later. What an old-fashioned girl I grew up to be!

There were traditional women's jobs in the mill: mending, burling, spinning and weaving, but these were mostly done by unmarried women, girls just out of school, the widowed, and the ones who were struggling to make ends meet because of illness in the family. Women did sewing, tailoring, dressmaking, cleaning, office work, served in shops. Even married women did this especially if the business was in the family. There were few professional women that I was aware of, except for nurses who generally were much respected and in demand in the community to sit through the night with the very ill, and to lay out the dead for burial. Women were teachers, of course, again, mostly spinsters. I remember Miss Iredale, Miss Whitely, Miss Milne, and unusually, dear Mrs Battye. It was said that her husband hated work, so he stayed home to mind the house and Nellie was the wage earner! Our Vicar's wife, Mrs Dangerfield, had a job, too. She taught English at the College in Huddersfield, and that mostly met with disapproval, as she was rarely available to attend the Mothers Union or the Young Wives group like a 'proper' vicar's wife! Lady doctors were few and far between. I can't recall any.

Women did work, of course. Housework and caring for a family was hard going in those days, with few of the modern appliances considered to be so essential fifty years later. Many women still cooked and baked for their family in a side oven, with no indication of the temperature except experience, open the door, put in a hand and declare it ready, or not, as the case may be. At Ivy Cottage the big range was taken out when I was about nine or ten years old, and Mam bought a secondhand tiled fireplace. Then we were left to use Mam's new electric cooker. It quickly proved inadequate, and we had a pan stand on the hearth, up against the fire, and the vegetables were usually boiled in soot blackened pans on the fire. Two pans could be accommodated in this way thus saving time and money; electricity was both slow and expensive. There was a boiler behind the fire for the hot water supply, so for washing or for baths, a fire had to be lit, even in the hottest of summers.

Fire lighting was something of a trial, especially on cold wet mornings when you wakened to a cold cheerless house with only cinders and ash in the grate, and on windy mornings when the smoke blew back into the room.

The ash tin had to be taken round to the dustbin to empty, braving the rain or the snow or the wind. Then several pieces of newspaper had to be rolled up and tied into knots. These were laid on the cleared grate, crisscrossed with dry sticks, and a few small pieces of coal laid on top. Then the matches, and a small flicker of flame would creep along the edges of the newspaper, and I would cross my fingers and hope that it would 'go'. Sometimes it did and that was wonderful and satisfying. Often it did not, it would smoulder dully and the coal would not 'catch'. Then, the draw tin being worn out, the shovel had to be put in front of the grate and a piece of newspaper put across it to create a good draught. Highly dangerous and on more than one occasion, the fire drew so well that the newspaper went up in flames too, but at least you knew you were going to get the house warm! Probably the nicest thing about a coal fire was when it burned fierce and red, usually on a frosty evening, and we made toast, using the long toasting fork which hung on the wall beside the fireplace: perhaps the most appetizing smell in the world.

Another job which I hated was 'cleaning out', cleaning the front steps and covering them with scouring stone. Mam favoured something called 'ruddle' stone; a large knobbly lump of, I suppose, sandstone, bright yellow in colour. We had a small galvanized bucket, kept under the sink, and a special piece of rag, and a scrubbing brush. A large cloth apron, tied over the usual pinafore, completed the equipment. It was a cold job, too public for my liking, and hard on the hands, but oh, so very important. What would the neighbours say if the steps were left dirty? We all knew exactly what the neighbours would say and it would not be complimentary! Pride must prevail at all costs.

Cooking and baking I enjoyed with Mam. Goodness knows how she managed it, but I think she and Grandma must have had stocks of sugar and dried fruit hoarded from before the war, as we always had Christmas Cake and Christmas Pudding, and plain cakes at other times. Yorkshire Pudding was the eternal favourite of course, rising until it 'knocked the top of the oven off'! Joints of meat were tiny and poor and yielded little in the way of dripping, so it was a treat to have bread and dripping with a sprinkling of salt for breakfast or tea.

Mam did have a vacuum cleaner, christened Josephine by me! After all, she was a young married woman with many of the 'mod-cons'. These included as well as the electric oven, an electric iron, superseding Grandma's flat iron, but no ironing board, the job was done on the table.

Washing was perhaps the greatest trial, for to begin with, Mam had just two large zinc tubs, one which had an extended side forming a rubbing board, and a hand wringer with rubber rollers. This was a great improvement on Grandma's mangle, which had wooden rollers and countless cogs and wheels, and a large handle. It was free standing and solid; a monster that was banished to the back of the wash kitchen when Mam's modern equipment moved in. When Grandma became very ill with a stroke, the laundry situation was pretty dire, until she decided to buy an electric washing machine for Mam. Wow! What a wonderful machine it was! It was large and square, with a powered wringer and a large agitator which turned back and forth to thoroughly clean the clothes, then, through the wringer they went into the tub of clean water (with a drop of ammonia to make the clothes soft) where once again, the posser had to be employed. This was a smooth disc of wood about eight inches in diameter, ridged underneath, and fixed on a long pole, and this was used to press the clothes up and down in the water; hard work indeed. Even with the new wonderful machine, buckets had to be used to fill and empty it, collars still had to be scrubbed, Dad's overall pockets had to be brushed clean of hair clippings, 'dolly blue' and starch had to be made in a bucket for shirts and pillow cases; such a performance, a whole day's job.

Add to these lengthy jobs the shopping, the making of meals and caring for the elderly and infirm, and a woman's life was very busy indeed, and children, like me, were expected to make their contribution, and help. Coupled with with these activities was the necessity

Figure 8.1
This was Grandma's
equipment for the weekly wash!

to, *'make do and mend'*. Children's clothes were made, often from adult clothes cut down; and woollies were knitted for winter from old hand knitted garments which had found their way to the jumble sale. They were bought for a few coppers, unravelled, sometimes re-dyed, and knitted up again. Thankfully, Mam was never quite so impoverished and almost always managed to buy new material or wool, but now and again one of her jumpers might be pulled back and re-knitted as a cardigan for me. It was War-time and ingenuity was much in evidence.

Mam had nursed Grandma for a considerable time, but eventually, she consented to go into hospital. I'm sure she could see the strain was too much for Mam. This then entailed visiting on Wednesday, Saturday and Sunday each week, for one hour only. It was a long, time consuming journey on the bus followed by a long walk.

This was the situation then, when Mam announced she had taken a part time job in the mill. Money was tight. Dad was out all day until very late, except for Wednesdays and Sundays. I was at school and old enough to get myself there without help. I must have been about ten or eleven years old. It caused a tremendous furore. Rows, arguments and upset went on for days - the shame and disgrace she was causing, but she prevailed and went as a burler to Bridge Mill in Holmfirth. She caught the 6.30 am bus and returned home at about 2.00 pm. Dad was furious and took it with very bad grace, but times were beginning to change.

'Latch key kids' were the product of more mothers going out to work and the topic received much publicity in the papers and on the wireless. As Mam's hours of work changed and a routine was established, I was somewhat dismayed to learn that I fitted that description to a small degree. I didn't feel myself to be hard done by at all, I rather enjoyed the independence which arriving home before Mam gave me, and we still enjoyed lovely evenings together, and one or two days each week, plus Saturdays and Sundays.

School holidays were the most worrying time for Mam, but I was a child who was happy to have her head in a book and sensible enough to be left in charge of the house. We lived in a very close community in Underbank, and I am sure the good friends and neighbours kept an eye on me. After all, those were the days when you popped out to the shop with no thought of locking the door, even sometimes, walking down to Holmfirth and leaving it unlocked. Sometimes the key could be left under the mat and on one notable occasion, Mam had to go out and was expecting the decorator (a nephew of Dad's) so she left a note on the door 'Decorator - key under mat!' Precious times, when everyone knew everyone else, and all were honest and neighbourly. Frequently, they were nosey too, but no person was allowed to be ill and alone, no old lady was found dead in bed after the milk had accumulated for days on the step.

During the school holidays, I would do the regular jobs around the house, make the beds, run the vacuum cleaner round, dust, wash up, read endlessly, take Wendy the dog out and play with my friends. I listened to the wireless a lot and made my routine around the programmes I enjoyed, and was glad when Mam arrived home early in the afternoon when we might go for a picnic, or go Blackberrying, or do the main jobs together. It must have been hard work for her, and much of the housework would still have to be tackled in the evening. I tried to keep things nice for her and sometimes it worked better than others. I was no saint and often spent most of my time reading and daydreaming. In winter, I always had to light the fire, of course. I can't imagine youngsters today being allowed to spend the day in such a manner, or indeed if I would have done such a thing with my boys. How times change, but I don't think it did me any harm: perhaps made me more self-reliant, used to my own company and content with myself. There was the day when she left me the money to go to the butcher for a bit of stewing meat- 'fry', we called it for some obscure reason. Must go in the morning or it would all be gone.

I looked at the meat and decided to make a pie for when she arrived home, have it all hot and ready for her and it would be a wonderful surprise. I had done it with her many times, so I cooked the meat with an onion, peeled the potatoes and some swede, and made the pastry.

Figure 8.2
Our little dog, Wendy

She was so impressed and surprised and we sat down and enjoyed it together, then, as we cleared up, she noticed the pie dish, just the right size for the two of us.

'Where did you find the dish, I don't remember us having one that size?'

'Oh that was easy,' I replied. 'It's the one we use for Wendy's dog biscuits. It's just right'. Well, she didn't know whether to laugh, cry or be cross! I seem to recall she did all three. She was thunderstruck.

'Well, I washed it first' was all I could say, and as far as I know, we suffered no ill consequences, but I never lived it down.

Another time, in the summer holidays, I decided to do the washing for her. After all, we had a splendid machine to do all the hard work, didn't we? It was a glorious day, sunny and warm, with just the right amount of breeze.

I went upstairs to the wash kitchen and started sorting the clothes as I had seen her do, filling the washer with the enamel bucket to the right level, filling the tub for the rinsing, and adding that vital splash of ammonia to keep the clothes soft. I guessed the amount of soap powder, and in went the whites. Then, being extra careful to switch off the agitator, I put everything through the wringer into the tub to rinse, and the next load went into the washer.

While they were being washed, I possed away at the rinsing, and then, through the wringer they went again, me watching my fingers and being very careful. I even scrubbed the collars, after a fashion, and starched the shirts and the pillow slips. Into the basket it all went and out into the garden to be pegged on the line.

My satisfaction and pride was immense as I watched them blowing in the breeze to dry, and by the time Mam came home, they were all folded in the laundry basket ready to iron. I was so pleased with myself. Mam nearly had a fit! She couldn't believe her eyes! Shock and disbelief registered in every part of her.

141

'But, but, how did you fill the washer? How did you man-age the wringer? She continued with, 'My goodness, you could have trapped your fingers in it, or caught your hair in it, like that woman in Holmfirth. She caught her hair in the wringer and it was pulled out by the roots, never grew again properly, right across her forehead! You might have been killed by the electricity!'

'But I wasn't, Mam. I'm OK. I was careful and it's all done now. It's all ready to iron.'

Once again, she was thunderstruck, and I was shattered, tired out after my hard day. I don't think I ever tackled it again. Maybe it was just too much, or maybe she forbade me.

I took long walks with Wendy, our little dog. She was good company and we covered a lot of ground together, along Dover Lane, through Washpit Mill yard and back along Choppards, or up Swan Lane to Damhouse and out towards Wards Banks.

Olwynne came to play sometimes, her mother also went out to work, and we enjoyed our never ending game of make-believe, but Margaret was my special friend, we shared a desk at school and she played Our Game best of all.

Margaret and I longed to go camping and have adventures out in the country, sleeping in a tent, making a fire and being out in the wild all night. We were both keen readers and were well into Enid Blyton, Malcolm Saville and Arthur Ransome. The likelihood of ever doing it was remote. Quite apart from parental disapproval, we had no tent and no money, and so we took to wishing at every opportunity.

The saying went that if you accidentally said the same words, at the same time, as another person, you could link your little fingers close your eyes and make a wish. Numberless times we contrived to speak together to 'qualify' and we wished most vigorously, all to no avail. We toyed with the idea of earning money, but neither Margaret's mother nor mine could afford to pay us for running errands, and on one hot day in summer we were playing in our garden and had the brilliant idea of selling bunches of flowers to the neighbours. We picked roses, marigolds, nasturtiums, cat mint, and bunched them up, and went round the neighbours, selling them for sixpence a bunch. Some we sold, other people turned us down and I put some of the leftovers in a vase and some Margaret took home. We had made, I suppose, about three shillings and sixpence. Not much, but a start. I said nothing about it to Mam as I had the distinct feeling she would not approve. How right I was! Very swiftly the grape vine came into action and someone told her of our exploits. She was so angry and mortified she made me give all the money back and promise never even to think of such a thing again. Bit by bit, the time went by and the idea of camping faded forever.

Before her marriage, Mam had worked as a mender in the mill, an extremely skilled job, but a dirty one as the cloth was handled straight from the loom and was still greasy. All the imperfections in the cloth had to be invisibly mended. When a shuttle had faltered or had to be renewed, the consequent long ends and missed weft had to be sewn in. If the loom itself had faltered and the 'healds' which governed the pattern of the warp had for some reason gone wrong, that too had to be made perfect. The cloth woven in Holmfirth mills was mostly fine worsted suitings, so the work required good eyesight as well as a nimble needle. The women worked in pairs sitting at a large table, always at a window for maximum light. It always intrigued me that the thimble used by the menders had no top, but was like a metal ring with strong indentations around the sides.

When Mam decided to go back to work, she felt her eye-sight eyesight may not be up to mending, so she went as a burler. This was much cleaner, the cloth had been scoured (washed) and was almost finished and ready to be sold. Burlers, like menders worked at a raised table, at a window, in pairs. They used a pair of sharp pointed tweezers, called burling irons, and their job was to remove any imperfections in the yarn. It was easier, cleaner and inevitably rated a lower wage. Mam had a lovely partner, Mary, and they worked very happily together and became good friends. Occasionally there were outings arranged from the mill, perhaps a coach trip to Blackpool or to Scarborough, and in this way Mam had more company and a new dimension was added to her life. I sometimes visited her at work during school holidays and I always found it interesting if rather frightening in the mill.

After Grandma's death, Mam moved from Bridge Mill to a small commission business on the second floor of Perseverance Mill. The man had, I think, six looms and a couple of mending tables, and Mam went back to being a mender. It was at Perseverance that she met an older lady, a widow called Rosetta. Rosetta was a weaver and on the occasions when I visited Mam at work there, I was allowed to stand at the loom, in the loom gate, and watch the cloth being woven. It was fascinating, and amazing to me that the shuttle passed back and forth with such speed that you couldn't see it! It is this movement of the shuttle that makes the noise, the clacking, clattering noise of the loom and it is said that six looms make as much noise as a whole weaving shed, but I don't know about that. Whether the looms that are used nowadays bear any likeness to the ones all those years ago, I have no idea. Sufficient to say, it was very noisy indeed, and dangerous. I was always made to stand in the safety of the loom gate, with the weaver, and never allowed to loiter at the side. No one did, for many were the tales of the shuttle missing its return and flying out, through the window and down into the mill dam! Many too, were the tales of men who had been killed by such a flying shuttle.

Rosetta lived at the top of a very steep hill in Holmfirth, in a small terraced house, and we visited her quite often. She had no electricity and the house had gas lighting. It was my first experience of this and the need to have a gas mantle which glowed incandescent in the heat and gave out a clear light. Sometimes the light waned and sometimes popped and hissed when the gas supply was uncertain. She also had a gas iron, a truly fearsome contraption. It was tall, and black, and the flames would lick out between the sole plate and the top. She held the handle with an asbestos cloth like a pan holder. I found it terrifying. I never offered to help with that particular job! Sometimes we went for tea in her little house and we would make toast. It was very cozy, sitting round the fire with the strange gas light hissing in the background.

The friendship gradually waned, however. Mam and Rosetta had had some difference of opinion, about what, I cannot recall, and Mam was very upset with her. She, rather unwisely as it turned out, told me what had been said. The next time I went to the mill, I saw Mam and then left without my usual greeting to Rosetta. After all, she had upset my mother. So, Rosetta was upset with me for ignoring her; Mam was upset with me for being rude to her friend; I was upset because my action had been to support, as I thought, my Mam! What a mess, and so the difference between them became a gulf and although mended on the surface, the friendship never really recovered.

CHAPTER NINE

Underbank

Underbank is a short walk from the centre of Holmfirth, and is built on one side of the valley of the smaller stream, the Ribble. Looking across from Ivy Cottage the view was of fields and woods, just a cluster of houses nestled together under the brow of the hill, at Damhouse, but if you took the path down from the main road, crossed over the little river and climbed the steep hill of Swan Lane, and then looked back, the hillside was full of houses, stacked one upon another! It was such a contrast, so startling, like turning the pages of a book, or coming out of a tunnel! In fact there seemed to be so many houses it was difficult to pick out Ivy Cottage. Mam and I would walk to the very top of the hill, purple with heather in July and August, taking with us a small pocket mirror. We would sit and flash the mirror in the sunshine and whoever we had left behind at home, Grandma, Grandad or Dad would signal back. It was so satisfying to see the light and then to pick out all the houses along Kippax Row; Cuttle Mill and its chimney; Auntie Beattie's house and Joan's below it.

During my early childhood the village was quite self-sufficient, and boasted a pub, a Co-op grocer and butcher, a cobbler, a baker, two fish and chip shops, a working men's club, a sweet shop-cum-newsagent, and a Wesleyan Chapel. It also had a telephone box, where you had to ask for the number and put four pennies in the slot when told to do so. When your call was connected you pressed Button A and had your conversation. If you could not be connected you pressed Button B and got your money back. Often we children would go and optimistically press Button B and very occasionally we were rewarded with four pence. Few people had a telephone, and I suspect it was used mainly for calling the doctor or the hospital.

Two buses served the village, one took the longer route to Huddersfield through the villages of Scholes and New Mill, and one, privately owned by a local firm, which went up to Hade Edge and thence over the moors to Penistone or Dunford Bridge.

Very importantly, there were three mills, which gave employment to most of the men and many of the women. Washpit was the largest, Dover Mill was quite small and almost hidden in the valley bottom , it had a dam with sheer concrete sides which gave my mother nightmares. It was quite unprotected and when the water was low, was a death trap for the careless. Cuttle Mill was away from the river, and in summer time, when the mill windows were open, you could just hear the faint clatter of the looms in our garden.

Mam, in common with many people in Underbank, had actually been born in the house in which we lived. Everyone knew everyone else, their parents, brothers, sisters, grandparents, aunts and uncles. Buses were infrequent and a trip to Holmfirth happened perhaps once a week, and a trip to Huddersfield some six miles away, was an event. Work was nearby in the mill, so every-one's idiosyncrasies, and they were many, were well known.

I soon grew to recognize the village folk, who all knew me, of course, as Connie's little girl. Their comment

148

when they saw me with Mam was 'Here comes Connie and little Connie'.

Our next door neighbour, Mrs Brook, always known as Mrs Harold, to identify which Mr Brook she was wife to, was a kindly soul, rosy cheeked and white haired, and always to be seen in a cross-over apron. However, word had it that they were such fierce supporters of the Labour Party that, given the chance, they would stand Mr Churchill up against a wall and shoot him!

Their home was well polished and cared for, and all the legs of the chairs and table were adorned with Mrs Harold's old stockings, to save them from getting kicked and scuffed! A rag rug, or as it was sometimes known, a peg rug or a list rug, lay in front of the fire, homemade, of course, from small pieces of cloth cut from old suits and jackets and threaded into a canvas base.

Many people had these and many evenings must have been spent in patiently cutting up the rug bits and forcing them into the canvas with a special tool. They were often very attractive and all were hard-wearing.

Next to Mrs Harold lived Mrs Booth, an elderly widow who lived alone and talked much about her sons Lionel and Elvin. She was a kind and lovely lady, but seemed to have acquired a reputation for fancying the men.....! She must have been well into her seventies, and when she bought herself a new coat one year which was bright fuchsia pink, well, the tongues wagged. Such an unsuitable colour for a woman of her age! Her reputation must be well deserved! Gossips in any community can be cruel and hurtful. To us she was always kind and a good friend.

Almost at the far end of Kippax Row lived Mary Ann, a huge old lady, who walked painfully to the shop once or twice a week. Winter and summer alike she wore a voluminous black coat, with two large buttons in front. It came down to her ankles. She had a pleasant homely face, with watery blue eyes and several chins. She would always stop to pass the time of day and I have sometimes seen her upset and almost tearful, her lip and chins quivering in distress. She spoke, like most of the elderly people there in very broad dialect, which fascinated me.

Above Ivy Cottage, on the 'top' road, lived Mam's friend, Kathleen; they had been friends since school days. She and her husband Edgar and sons Douglas and Alton (yet another unusual name), who, it was said, would never again be the same since he was rescued from the beaches of Dunkirk. Not until many years later did I appreciate the full import of that statement. Dunkirk to me was just another place name. They were not as fortunate as us and had no bathroom. The old zinc bath had to be brought in from the wash house and filled from the boiler beside the fire in the old range, and afterwards emptied, sometimes down the steps into the road! Edgar played bass in Hade Edge Band and we had many excursions with them to band contests over the moors in Lancashire. I clearly remember visiting them one day when they had just received a box full of day-old chicks. The sheer wonder of taking the lid off the box and all the chicks 'coming to life' in the light, and cheeping away! It was marvellous to me. Somewhere up in the back garden they must have had a hen run, but I was never lucky enough to see it.

Just across Kippax Row lived my great friend Anita. We spent many happy hours playing together, in our garden or hers. She was two years older than me and looking back now, I think she probably took the lead in most of our games. We went to Church and to Sunday School together and both attended 'National' School, although Anita was always early and I was mostly late, running down Pop Alley (the short cut) and Dunford Road as if my very life depended on it. She told me once that my teacher had asked her to tell me that I was needed to give out the pencils and help her to get the classroom ready, so would I be at school for ten minutes to nine? I made a tremendous effort and arrived next morning at ten to nine and went up to the classroom. It was quite empty, pencils on the desks in readiness. I was baffled. Later, she confessed that she was only trying to help me to be more punctual! Alas, her efforts were in vain, punctuality remained a problem!

Anita's mother, Clara, was a lovely lady, large and beaming, with big eyes and a fine sense of drama when she told us a tale. She and Mam had been at school and grown up together. She was kindness itself to us, and many years later, when I was working and Mam was in hospital, I arrived home at about two o'clock on the Wednesday, my half day, to find a cardboard box on the doorstep. It contained a small meat and potato pie and a jar full of gravy, still hot! I always remember her kindness, I wonder if she ever realised what it meant to me. She was married to Ernest who was the manager of the Co-op grocers in Underbank. For some reason, Mam was not registered with them but I was still sent there on errands from time to time. Sometimes the word went round that they had some butter there, and I would be dispatched to buy half a pound. It was usually Finnish tub butter and it stood on the mahogany counter while the wooden segments of the tub were removed one by one and the butter cut into portions, weighed and priced and wrapped in grease proof paper.

Down on the main road lived Ada Annie (pronounced always with the intrusive 'r' at the end of Ada) and her husband Jack. They were large people, tall, stout, heavy. Ada Annie, always attired in floral finery, had no ambition to move away from her mother, and presumably, Jack felt the same. The three of them lived happily in the small cottage, which gave straight on to the pavement. Ada Annie loved her Jack and packed his sandwiches every day for him to take to the mill, maybe a teacake with jam for breakfast and a similar teacake with cheese or boiled ham or Spam for his dinner. Jack invariably ate the ham for breakfast and the jam for dinner on the basis that he might die before dinner time and never get to eat it.

Most people who lived on the main road made a great show of sweeping out and keeping their patch of pavement clean. *'Cleanliness is next to Godliness'* was an often heard maxim. Odd superstitions prevailed, too; one I remember made it necessary to put the children's offerings of bluebells or buttercups into a jar and put it on the outside window sill, it being considered very unlucky to have them in the house! Can't think why or where that came from. It was not a superstition that prevailed at Ivy Cottage, I'm glad to say.

My friend Olwynne lived on Low Side and she too enjoyed games of make believe. Olwynne went to dancing class and I remember being quite envious of the costumes she wore, the pretty tap and ballet shoes and the lovely ringlets which her mother styled into her hair for her classes and concerts. Another school friend was Marlene, to whose birthday party I was invited, when she was about nine years old, and we ate a tinned fish in sandwiches called Snoek. I can't remember much about the taste, most things were acceptable to me, but Mam was somewhat taken aback when I told her. Food, of course, was mostly still rationed, but Snoek apparently, was not. Why Mam had never tried it I don't know, but I reckon she found the name unappealing! In later years Marlene married and went to live in the house at the end of our garden, the one with the window which Grandad had built the greenhouse against.

There were, inevitably, several large, poor families; they had many children, little money. One family lived right next door to the school, and during the time when Mam worked at Bridge Mill, she became friendly with a young girl and her family, Brenda. When Brenda married, the house next to the school became vacant and they were set to move in. What a scrubbing and clearing out of rubbish, a job for the stout hearted and no mistake! The house had to be 'stoved' which meant burning sulphur candles in all the rooms, shutting the doors and windows and leaving it all night in order to get rid of all the bugs, but when all was done, the rooms newly painted and papered, it made a lovely home for the newly-weds! Another notorious family was that of the local rag and bone man. He had a horse and cart with his name painted on - Wright Sanderson, known locally as 'Shink'. He also had many children, who were quite beautiful under the grime, and rumour had it that in the cottage in South Lane, where they lived, he had taken up all the flagstones in the living room, and the children played in the corner, digging at the hard impacted earth and making a puddle in the hollow they had created.

Two other characters spring to mind. Charlie Stubbins lived right out on the moors above Hade Edge; a bleak place even in the height of summer. Hade Edge was a small cluster of houses, a shop, a chapel, the Bandroom, and a pub called The Bay Horse. Some distance from this

Figure 9.1
Charlie Stubbins

village was the hamlet of Magnum, which had a tiny church, seating about twelve people. Fairly near at hand were two farm houses which lay derelict and windswept. One was called Hades (pronounced like spades) and the other was Elysium. Elysium was dismantled after the War and the stone used to build the new Working Men's Club in Underbank, lovely stone, a mellow pale gold. Somewhere in this inhospitable place, Charlie lived rough, with his dog, and would occasionally be seen in Holmfirth, a slight, grey haired, bearded figure in an old dark overcoat, tied at the waist with string. He had a gentle, kindly countenance, and I shocked Mam once by saying I thought he looked like Jesus!

Firth Lee was another old gentleman, very different to Charlie in that he was tall and well-built, with a a splendid moustache and a wide-brimmed hat, very flamboyant. His tattered waistcoat sported a watch chain, and he wore and he wore a red neckerchief and a patched and threadbare coat.

I have no idea where he lived, but he would appear, like Charlie, from time to time, especially in winter, when his need of food and shelter was very great.

Figure 9.2
Firth Lee

Trevor Bray, who had a photographic studio, would sometimes take photographs of them and sell the reprints in his shop, to raise money for them.

Both men had chosen to live as tramps, and were cared for with rough haphazard kindness by the local people.

CHAPTER TEN

Visits and Visitors,
High Days and Holidays

Mam kept in touch with her friends by letter, and by visiting, usually for tea. It would have been a Saturday when we visited Alice, who had been a good friend for many years. She had never married, and had lovely grey eyes set quite wide apart in a face which seemed to reveal nothing of her feelings, no animation at all. She lived in Jackson Bridge, a short bus ride away, in a small terrace house on the main road. On the other side of the road flowed the little river, clear and strong with a small waterfall which could be heard tumbling and roaring even in Alice's front room.

Three generations lived there, and when Alice's sister Gladys visited with her baby, there were four generations under the same roof. For some reason this fascinated me, I quite overlooked the fact that three generations lived in our house! Old Mrs Hinchliffe was small with a double chin which quivered. She spoke in very broad Yorkshire dialect and I loved to listen to her. I could well be mistaken, but I think she was approaching ninety, a tremendous age in those days. If we arrived early and went, as always, to the back door, we would probably find Mr Hinchliffe, Alice's father, getting washed and shaved at the kitchen sink, and her mother, dressed always in dark brown, with an apron, bustling about the kitchen preparing tea while

Gran sat beside the fire. I once remarked to Mam that it was a shame they did not have a bathroom like us, and she replied to my astonishment that they did! At some point she had been shown around the house and the bathroom was proudly revealed to her, gleaming and spotlessly clean; the towels arranged on the rail were decorated with about six inches of beautiful hand-worked crochet, but it was never used, unless perhaps the doctor had to make a visit, and he was allowed to wash his hands there. They all continued to perform their toilet downstairs and to visit the outside lavatory across the back yard, under the shadow of the steep hillside. They were, however, very homely and hospitable people and I enjoyed going to tea there. Perhaps the highlight of the visit was actually the last quarter- hour or so when Alice, Mam and I would go into the front room to wait for the bus. The front door opened directly on to the road and from that vantage point we could see the bus as it came down the hill, and we had just time to kiss goodbye and walk the few yards to the stop. The front room, like the bathroom, was never used except for this little ritual and it was cold, even in the middle of summer. The scent of mothballs, which delicately perfumed the entire house, was particularly strong in there. The floor was of scrubbed flagstones, with various lovely homemade rugs, and the chairs were upholstered in dark green velvet, each wearing its embroidered antimacassar. They were very uncomfortable. More uncomfortable still was the Victorian sofa, or chaise longue, which was horse hair and prickled the backs of my legs dreadfully when I sat on it. The other furniture was heavy, dark, richly-carved and polished.

On the sideboard stood an ornate clock and two arrangements of artificial flowers, each under a glass dome;

Figure 10.1
Christine with Auntie Jessie's son,
and Wendy the dog

there were tall vases on the mantelshelf, reflected in the large mirrored overmantel. There were other mirrors, too, with pictures painted on them so the usable space was quite restricted. The other pictures were of Highland cattle and mountains, all rather dark and gloomy, in heavy frames; and pictures which had been made of different coloured pieces of silver paper, usually a crinoline lady, stuck on to a black background. The table at the other end of the room was covered in knick-knacks, the best of which, in my opinion, was a bronze dog. When you lifted his tail you could place a nut between his jaws and crack it! Wonderful! Mam said it would never work, it was just for fancy. Thinking now of the houses which have been taken over by the National Trust, it seems a pity they never heard of Alice's family home. It was a positive treasure trove of Victoriana and Edwardian style. I found it fascinating and I am sure other people would have enjoyed it's 'time warp' quality

Mam and I occasionally visited Auntie Jackman who used to live next door to us in Lockwood. She was a good friend and neighbour to Mam, and had two boys, Bernard and Eric.

About the time we moved to Ivy Cottage they moved to an-other area of Huddersfield – Lindley - and it was quite an expedition to visit them. I would play with the boys in the garden, on their bikes, or with their clockwork train set, which had a tunnel, and their Bagatelle.

Eric, who was the youngest, could add up the score like lightning and would grow very excited, adding everyone's score and rushing us on to the next turn. I found it quite off-putting, I must say, arithmetic never coming easy to me. They had a fireplace with a side oven, although Auntie Jackman had a gas cooker, and the side oven was only used to keep things warm, be it clothes, towels or just firewood. They also had a black cat and one day we arrived to find everyone very sad. The cat had crept into the oven where it was warm and settled himself on the towel that was there. Unfortunately, someone in a fit of tidiness shut the oven door and it was some hours before his mews were heard and he was released. The poor creature never recovered and died soon after.

Inviting friends and family to tea, and being invited in return, was the accepted way of socializing and keeping in touch, and we often had company for Sunday tea. It was 'High Tea', and the more significant the day, the 'higher' it got! It was an event. One of Mam's best table-cloths must be chosen and the best china brought from the sideboard in the sitting room. The table had to be fully opened, which took a great deal of space in our small living room. Everything had to be prepared in good time so that everyone was washed and changed into best clothes before the company arrived. It was a substantial meal, as I remember it. First would be some kind of cold meat and pork pie. When times were bad it would be some tinned preparation such as 'Spam' or corned beef, which Dad referred to as 'poorly monkey' and which Mam was rarely allowed to buy, his opinion of it being so low! In winter this would be accompanied by pickles: onions, beetroot, red cabbage, or chutney, mostly home-made. In summer it would be served with salad, and certainly in Grandad's day there would be Webb's Wonderful lettuce, crisp and crinkly, with 'white icicle' radishes, so hot they burnt your tongue, and cucumber, and delicious tomatoes from the greenhouse. Always there was bread and butter, well, margarine, and two pieces must be eaten with the meat. Following this came scones or Sally Lunn, and then, and not until then, jelly or blancmange, or fruit and cream. Tinned pears or peaches were the favourites for me, and pears were best of all. The 'cream' would be cold custard or tinned evaporated milk. I always refused the cream, saying it spoiled the taste of the pears! (I had always sucked my finger from being very small, and received a good deal of teasing about this unfortunate habit, but when asked what it tasted of I always replied 'juicy pears'). After the fruit you could have a piece of cake, homemade sponge cake or on special days, fruit cake. Quite a ritual was High Tea, when you had company on Sundays!

Dad's sister, Auntie Phyllis and Uncle Frank came to tea quite often, and they were the nicest of our visitors. Uncle Frank was a lovely, kindly man, full of fun and quite willing for me to tease and play with him. Auntie Phyllis was lovely too, but a bit austere and formal, and it was not until many years later that I appreciated how soft hearted she really was. We visited them, too, of course, and on those occasions I had to be on my very best behaviour; no elbows on the table, don't talk with your mouth full, remember your p's and q's, don't fidget, keep your knife and fork on your plate!

The other people I recall visiting were Auntie Jessie and Uncle Ernest, a courtesy title as they were in no way related to us. They lived in Honley and it was an interesting journey; walk to Holmfirth, bus to Honley, walk up through the old village, passed the well, and out to the newer houses beyond. Tea followed more or less the same pattern, although I fear not quite so lavish as at Ivy Cottage! And the fruit was always, without fail, stewed prunes and custard, served in white china bowls with a knobbly gold line around the edge. Auntie Jessie had a beautiful white Shelley china tea service, with square plates and deeply fluted cups. So deeply fluted were they, that when you looked down on a cup of tea, it was the shape of a flower. Mam was always careful to instruct me to drink my tea from the place where the edge of the cup curved out, towards my mouth, otherwise I might spill it. I grew resentful at this repeated instruction. After all, I wasn't a baby, I could drink perfectly well, why the fuss? So, one day, I drank from the part that went in towards the centre of the cup, with the inevitable result, tea all down my frock and onto the tablecloth! I was mortified, so embarrassed, and had to be mopped up and told off! Somehow, the Shelley china didn't seem quite so beautiful after that.

The real centre of social activity for us was Church. Mam was a member of the Mothers' Union and the Young Wives' Group, and I was a member of the Girls' Friendly Society, the GFS, and there I met all the girls I knew at Sunday school. We met in the Church Vestry on Tuesday evenings and played games like charades, did country

161

dancing and fancy skipping. Somehow we never seemed to be considered good enough to take part in the Annual Rally in Mirfield. Maybe there weren't enough of us. We used to go along there and see other groups performing and it never thrilled us very much as it made us feel very out of things. The best thing about GFS was when I was allowed three pence to buy some chips on the way home. Mavis, my friend there, always had the money and we would go together for our three penn'orth, with lots of salt and vinegar and wrapped in newspaper. Mavis's theory was that when you held them in your hand you should squeeze them gently and then the salt and vinegar went right into the chips and made them even more delicious. If you squeezed too hard, they all squashed together, so there was a good deal of skill and judgement involved!

We had a Sunday school trip in the summer and that was a big excitement. All the bustle of making sandwiches and wrapping them up in greaseproof paper, plus a slice of cake or a couple of biscuits, maybe a packet of crisps with a small screw of salt in dark blue waxed paper in amongst the crisps, all ready to be sprinkled. Sometimes Mam took the old thermos flask, even though it made the tea taste funny; I must wear my sandals, take a cardigan in case it was cold, my bathing costume and a towel, and my pocket money. What if it should rain? Should I take my bucket and spade? That was all right if the outing was to Blackpool which has lovely sands and waves, but more often than not we went to Southport, and the sea at Southport is a very, very long way out. Each year we would hope the tide would be in, so that we could paddle, but in or out, we never managed to walk to the sea. It was like a mirage on the far horizon; miles and miles of sand and a thin blue line of sea in the distance which never got any nearer. Why Southport, we asked? It was said the vicar had friends there but, whether that was true, I don't know. At all events, we enjoyed our day out. All too soon it was time to go back to the bus, rosy cheeked and windblown, sandals and socks full of sand and clutching our souvenirs, the present for Grandma and the stick of rock for Dad. We sang at the tops of our voices all the way home.

The most special of all trips with the Mothers' Union was to London during the summer of 1948. I was just ten years old. The event was The Mothers' Union World-Wide Conference, and it was to be held in the Westminster Hall. The speaker was to be Field-Marshal The Viscount Montgomery of Alamein. By some wonderful chance, our Mothers' Union was invited to be part of the choir, formed from groups like ours from all over the country. It was a great honour and a great responsibility. The music was chosen by the organizers and each choir had to obtain their own copies. One caused a problem, 'The Spinning Wheel', but it was eventually located in the County Music Library in Wakefield. Rehearsals began in good time and the hard work commenced. Week after week the ladies went to practice until the choirmaster, Arthur Coates, was satisfied, and plans were made for the wonderful trip.

It was during this time that the swimming pool in Holmfirth was re-opened, and my class at school was able to have swimming lessons. The weather was cold and I went along with my bathing costume and an old rain hood, swimming hats were well-nigh unobtainable. I had never been in water up to my chest before and I was shocked and scared as the water took my breath away. I hung on to the rail for dear life, shivering, and my teeth chattering. Then, being told to let go the rail, I did, and floundered around, my feet came up, my head went under and I panicked. The teacher, who was dark haired, thin, in a checked coat and a scarf, bellowed out, 'Look at that silly girl! Come back to the side at once!'

I was busy swallowing the pool and going down for the third time! Somehow, I survived that lesson and the following week, in spite of a strange pain in my tummy, we were on our way to London. I was the only child to go, Mam being the only one to take up the offer of taking a child with them.

I have a confused jumble of memories from that visit; the very long train journey, and my first sight of a London street; so wide, so many cars and taxis and buses, and so difficult to cross. The buildings were high and the colours quite different to home - whitish, greyish stone. The street noise seemed deafening and never stopped. It roared me to sleep and was still roaring when I woke up next morning. The Underground was good, especially the stations that were really deep and had a long escalator, or maybe even two. I was thrilled and excited by the noise and the speed of the trains, and the wind that each train brought, and the command 'Mind the doors'

It was Mam's intention to visit Mr Hiscock, our old gentle-man evacuee, and he lived in the East End, in Plaistow. It seemed a long way and I reckon Mam was very brave to venture that distance alone, armed only with his letter, and a few written instructions from a friendly London bobby. We walked and walked for ages, along dirty streets, and passed wide open areas of waste ground which, up to the Blitz, had been rows of houses. Mam said it really brought home to her the devastation of the war, but we found the place! We found dear Mr Hiscock and his family, and were made so very welcome. It was arranged that he would meet us the following morning and while Mam was with the choir for the rehearsal and the big festival, he and I would spend the day together. He was so gentle and kind and I remember he took me on a boat down the river from Westminster Pier and showed me all the sights. It was cold and windy although it was July.

The pain in my tummy persisted and the next day Mam took me to Charing Cross Hospital. The doctors were very nice and prodded my tummy and asked lots of questions. It was a bleak room, small white tiles from floor to ceiling, with large gaps in between, rather like a public convenience. We came away with a bottle of minty white medicine and instructions to see our family doc-tor when we arrived home. Mam rang Dad at the shop to tell him and later we discovered that in her anxiety for me, and the unfamiliar business of making a trunk call, the en-velope with all her music, including the precious Spinning Wheel song, which had never been sung as no other group had been able to obtain a copy, was lost! She must have left it in the phone box, but which phone box? Together with her friends, we visited every phone box in the vicin-ity of the Hotel but with no luck. Eventually, she reported the loss to a policeman and we returned home on the train with a turmoil of emotions; elation at the event, joy at see-ing Mr Hiscock again, concern about me and my tummy and guilt at losing the precious music.

When we arrived home the doctor was called in and announced that I had jaundice, probably caught at the swimming pool, and I was not to go swimming again. I was so pleased at that bit of news that I didn't really mind too much about being ill, except that I was forbidden all fats, and bread without butter and tea without milk were a bit dismal.

All in all, in spite of the jaundice, the trip had been very successful. Mam was thrilled to have been part of such an important event, to have sung with all the other choirs in the Central Hall, Westminster, and to have heard the almost legendary Monty address the meeting. I had visited the capital city of our country, and felt its power, it's very special atmosphere. I had seen the sights, Tower Bridge, Big Ben, Buckingham Palace, and been on the River Thames. We had met with dear Mr Hiscock again and that had been lovely, but Mam felt he had aged a lot since he had left us. We never heard from him again. Then one day there was a letter from his sister, to say he had passed away.

The train journey had been amazing. I loved trains. I loved watching them go by. I loved, as a very young child, to stand on the iron bridge that crossed the track and be enveloped in the smoke, clutching Mam's hand. It was so scary; so wonderful when it cleared. I loved seeing them go over the viaduct, with their plume of smoke trailing behind them; and the noise as they drew away from the station, the great gusts of steam like a giant breathing in anger. They were always dirty, Mam said, and smelled of smoke and soot, but trains to me meant holidays and excitement and going places. After the London trip I took out the old atlas that Grandad and I had looked at together, and found the names of the towns we had passed through.

Although times were still hard after the War, Mam managed to take me on holiday. Trains were there now for everyone, not just soldiers going or returning from leave. The beaches were being cleared of barbed wire and life was beginning to return to normal. We went to the East Coast, to Redcar, Saltburn, and Filey. I can only really remember Filey, and that not too clearly. We went with a friend of Mam's, called Ida, and her two children. Brenda was slightly older than me and Rodney a little bit younger. Dad could never go because of work and I suppose Ida's husband was in the same situation.

We all piled on to the train at Huddersfield Station, and we three children leaned out of the window to make the compartment seem full and unattractive to other travellers. Rodney pulled silly faces and Brenda and I considered borrowing Mam's lipstick and dotting our faces with red as if we had measles. We never did it, of course. It was good and reassuring for Mam to have company on the journey, as some trains still ran with entirely separate compartments, no corridor, and therefore, once you were moving there was no communication with any other travellers, and no escape from any undesirable character. There was always the Communication Cord, of course, which would stop the train in an emergency, 'Penalty for improper use - £5', but there was safety in numbers, and thankfully, such trains were becoming the exception.

The carriages were all beautifully panelled in lovely polished woods, with a kind of label telling you that it was walnut or maple, oak or elm. There were framed photographs, in black and white or sepia, of British castles and famous towns and resorts. To open the window you had to pull on a thick leather strap with holes in it like a belt, which disappeared inside the panelling of the door. We children couldn't manage to work it and we always clamoured to have the windows open and were never allowed because of the smoke and the small cinders from the engine which might blow into the train. Tunnels were great and we stared into the blackness of the windows, seeing our reflection there. Sometimes the lights dimmed, flickered and then went out for a few minutes. That was even better. If you were travelling alone in one of the isolated compartments and that happened it would have been very frightening indeed.

Filey, in those days was quite a small fishing town with a wide and beautiful beach. For me it was pure joy to run over the ridged and rippled golden sand down to the sea; to run along the shore and pick up the long strap-like lengths of seaweed and trail them behind me, the wind blowing my hair and making our voices sound thin and distant as we shouted at each other in our excitement We searched the rock pools for crabs and shrimps, touched the small sea anemones with our spades to make them close their tentacles, and climbed over the rocks on Filey Brig. We made castles and sand pies, dug holes, buried each other, and ran and ran in the space and the wind in exhilaration. There were shells to collect, and smooth pebbles, and bladder wrack seaweed to take home and hang outside the door to predict the weather. We went for a whole week, and a week was an eternity of delights.

Only once do I remember Mam taking me by herself, and that sticks in my mind because when we arrived at our boarding house, Mam could not find the Ration Books. And Ration Books were vital. Without them the landlady could not buy food for us, so she was not at all pleased. Mam searched the case, and her handbag, and did it again, and still they did not turn up. She was so upset and had to go to the Police Station to report their loss. Again she went through her large and sensible handbag to no avail. Sunday passed, and Monday and things were getting really desperate. We would have to cut our holiday short and go home. Once again she went through all the pockets of her bag ,and there they were! Unbelievably, they had been safely tucked in there all the time.

Mam vowed never to use that bag again and never to buy another one with so many pockets. The holiday was saved, but Mam's pride and self-esteem were damaged to a degree.

As I grew a little older, nine or ten, I suppose, Mam took me to the theatre. Huddersfield boasted two theatres at that time: the Palace, which was mostly variety, and best of all, the Theatre Royal. There was pantomime of course, but there were also plays, opera and operetta, both amateur and professional. The first play I ever saw was 'The Snow Queen' from the story by Hans Andersen. I think a group of us must have gone together from school, and we sat in the stalls, three rows from the front in the red plush tip-up seats, and expecting that it would start with an Opening Chorus like the pantomimes I had seen! I was enthralled, swept away by the story of Kay and Gerda, shedding tears when Gerda finds Kay and he is under the spell of the Snow Queen, and more tears when he was released and the happy ending was reached. It was magical, a world of enchantment. I was bewitched.

Mam loved music and whenever she could manage it she took me to the Theatre Royal. We saw 'Lilac Time' about Schubert; Ivor Novello's operettas 'Glamourous Night' and 'The Dancing Years'; Rossini's 'The Barber of Seville' and 'The Desert Song' and 'The Merry Widow'. We also occasionally went to the cinema in Holmfirth and I distinctly recall being taken to see Lawrence Olivier in 'Hamlet'. I found it gloomy and depressing, not to say baffling. What was it all about? The seeds of interest were sown and in due course, grew and flourished, and blossomed into my involvement with the local dramatic society, and with my elocution teacher, dear Ella Hirst.

CHAPTER ELEVEN

Holmfirth Amateur Dramatic Society

It was a glorious Saturday in early June, sunny and warm. The year was 1951, the war well and truly over, and the Festival of Britain in full swing. In London, the Skylon was drawing the crowds and proving a great attraction, and throughout the length and breadth of the land, festivities and celebrations were being enjoyed by young and old, with galas, games and parties for the children, old folks' treats, street parties and bunting; new buildings opening and memorial plaques being unveiled.

The Holme Valley was no exception, and the first Honley Show of peacetime was blessed with a perfect day, with all the excitement and bustle that such occasions bring. One of the many local bands was there, sporting gold braided uniforms, and in the arena there was show jumping and the judging of prize animals: cows, bulls, sheep and pigs. There were side shows, coconut shies, darts and roundabouts.

There was a Tea Tent, and a tent with flowers and vegetables, all arranged symmetrically and displaying their prize tickets, 'Best in Show', 'Highly Commended', 'Novice Class, First Prize'. It was never 'could do better'!

The air was sweet with the scent of the fresh flowers, cool and dim, away from the excitement out of doors, the passionate heat of competition hidden from the gaze of the spectators wandering in to the shade away from the dazzling sunshine for a few quiet moments.

Twice on that sunny day, the Holmfirth Amateur Dramatic Society were to present their play, 'Th'Owd Days' on a flat-bed lorry loaned by one of the local mills. It was a kind of 'mini-pageant' depicting scenes from the history of the valley, the move from hand weaving to the opening of the mills and the mechanized looms; the days of the Luddites, meeting in secret on the moors; the two terrible floods when Bilberry Reservoir burst its banks and the river swept away much of the town, and the second flood only seven years ago. It was written by a local playwright, George Taylor, and was designed for the very small stage. The cast and all props and scenery were to be carried on the wagon to various stopping places all over the Holme Valley, and the first two performances were to be at the Honley Show.

At the age of thirteen I was a junior member of the Dramatic Society and together with three of the boys, John, Tony and Neil, I was in the Mumming Play in one of the scenes. There were the usual characters: Bold Slasher (that was Tony) Gallant St. George (that was John) the Doctor (that was Neil,) and Father Christmas, and I was Father Christmas!

> *'Welcome or welcome not,*
> *I hope old Father Christmas*
> *Will never be forgot'*

It was great fun, and I sported a splendidly life-like beard of white crepe hair, attached to my face with spirit gum, my eyebrows rendered white with greasepaint applied the 'wrong' way, wonderful. In my full length hooded robe, my disguise would fool anyone, but, oh dear, on a hot summer day? Everyone else could change out of their costume between performances and look around the show, go and explore the delights of the Tea Tent and try their hand at the various competitions, but I couldn't change out of my red coat, unless I didn't mind appearing as the bearded lady!

Figure 11.1
The wagon show, 'Th'owd Days', for the Festival of Britain in
1951
Christine as Father Christmas, with Auntie Elsie

So I was confined to the back of the wagon, out of sight, with my hood down in the heat, and my friends brought me sandwiches and cakes and ice cream, and we picnicked there, in private, secretly, unseen except for one small boy who came to gaze in awe, and was quickly whisked away by his Mum.

The play was well received and during the following week we did two shows each evening at different places, Upperthong, Netherthong, Thongsbridge, Jackson Bridge, Scholes, Hepworth, all the surrounding villages, performing at different public houses and crossroads. It was wonderful and we were blessed with fine weather.

It was quite an undertaking, as we carried everything with us, chairs and benches for our audience, props and scenery for the play, the whole cast plus director and stage manager. Of course everyone had to give a hand in setting up and packing up. As we approached each stopping place, Uncle George our Town Crier, attired in his velvet coat and knee breeches, tricorn hat and buckled shoes, would walk ahead to announce our arrival and the time of the performance, ringing his bell and crying 'Oyez, Oyez' in time-honoured fashion.

Then came the final packing up and the ride back into Holmfirth in the rosy dusk, tired, happy, in good company; everyone singing together, and often the song was 'The Lord's my Shepherd' to the tune of Crimond. This was always Auntie Elsie's request, as it was her favourite.

Because of my make-up, I usually had to be there early and was often almost the last to leave, and as the week progressed, so did the stubborn spots of spirit gum on the sides of my face! It was fearsome stuff. Quite what happened to homework that week I can't remember for although we youngsters were in only one scene, we spent the rest of the time behind the wagon playing Checks (or Fivestones) often using the little stones we found on the ground and only after a couple of days acquiring a proper set from a shop. After a week of such intense practice we were undisputed champions!

How many miles we travelled, I don't know, but we went up hill and down dale, to as many of the small villages as possible. Most of the roads were narrow and steep, but fortunately we had no mishaps, nothing and no one fell off our wagon and we travelled triumphantly on, through the glorious countryside, passed woods carpeted with bluebells, beech trees in their new pale green, horse chestnut trees with their creamy spires of flowers; through mill yards and over the river, the sun warm and the evening breeze gentle and refreshing.

The contact with the Dramatic Society led to many pleasurable experiences and came as a result of Mam's friend, Elsie Houghton, and her husband, George. Mam and Elsie had been at school together and she, inevitably for a child with few near relations became Auntie. She was a very talented and accomplished actor and raconteur and had appeared in several plays with the Society which had won in the Northern Drama League competitions.

There were two major productions each year, in the Civic Hall, which was the nearest thing to a theatre in Holmfirth. It was a large, bare hall with a steeply raked stage, which was relatively small when scenery and props had to be accommodated. Between the two productions there were many social get-togethers at various people's homes. We had regular play readings and green room shows. They were a lovely group of people and at least two of the men wrote plays which were performed in Holmfirth, and one or two of which were published. A talented crowd! On several occasions they all came to Ivy Cottage for tea; and we joined them often at Auntie Elsie's home for eats of one kind or another.

Mam was well aware of my love of acting and I was doing well with my Elocution lessons with Ella Hirst. Sadly there are not many suitable plays with parts for very young girls, and I had to wait until I was sixteen before

I appeared in an Autumn production of 'Pink String and Sealing Wax' by Roland Pertwee.

The year after the excitement and fun of the Festival of Britain, 1952, saw the death of King George VI. I remember it clearly. No one had a television set in those days, the radio was all important, and on that day all the normal programmes were suspended, and replaced with solemn music which was occasionally interrupted by the announcement that the King had died. It was very gloomy and Mam and I were sitting at home in the quiet, missing our usual evening's entertainment, when suddenly there was an almighty crash and the sound of falling masonry on the landing and down the stairs! We were petrified, shocked, alarmed. When we cautiously opened the stairs door, the steps were full of rubble and a cloud of dust almost blocked our view. A portion of the ceiling above the landing had fallen in, caused, we thought by a blockage in the valley gutter between the bathroom and the rest of the house. What a mess! We no longer missed the entertainment. We had entertainment enough cleaning up!

The death of the King led to the crowning of the Queen, and once more, the local dramatists stepped in with a grand, full blown pageant 'The Voice of the Valley, to be presented in the Civic Hall. This was a mammoth undertaking involving two choirs, the Hade Edge Band, and a large cast of players. The whole was held together by two narrative characters, 'Spirit of the Past' and 'Spirit of the Present'.

Each scene had two halves, downstage was the scene from the past, and upstage, the scene at the present time. It was very clever and very effective, but, oh what a squash on the small stage, and what tremendous organization was needed to keep track of everyone and be sure all the choir members knew exactly where they should be, and when, and the band knew, and the players were also well informed.

The scene in which I took part, with Beryl, June, Mary and Betty was dated about 1860, when 'Pratty Flowers', the Holmfirth Anthem, was written by a local young man, Joe Perkin, to serenade his young lady.   We girls were all to be in crinolines, and with long ringlets.

Figure 11.2
"The Voice of the Valley"
produced for the Queen's Coronation. Christine on the left, all of us showing off our crinolines. The scene   depicted the first performance of the Holmfirth Anthem, 'Pratty Flowers'

176

The second half of the scene was the Male Voice Choir singing the song,

'Abroad for pleasure as I was a-walking
It was one summer, summer's evening clear
O there I beheld a most beautiful damsel
Lamenting for her shepherd dear.
'Wilt thou go fight yon French and Spaniards
Wilt thou leave me thus my dear?'
'No more to yon green banks will I take thee
With pleasure for to rest thyself and view the lambs,
But I will take thee to yon green garden
Where the pratty, pratty flowers grow
Where the pratty, pratty flowers grow.

Excitement grew as the date approached, all the scenes were put together, and we began to see the pageant as a whole. Excitement and anxiety, where were they to find so many costumes, funds, as always were stretched to the limit; how were all the musicians to be accommodated in the very restricted space? Carpenters and handy men were recruited to build an extension to the stage; all the trunks, cupboards and boxes which constituted the wardrobe were turned out and all the cast asked to bring anything from home which might conceivably be altered and used in some way.

Our scene needed some thought. Dresses long enough and wide enough in the skirt were found, but only one real crinoline. Ingenuity was needed to create the right effect and four out of the five of us were supplied with contraptions of two garden hoops, a large and a small, tied together with tape, which supported the skirt and looked most effective, and we strutted and paraded in our lovely dresses with some pride. Until, that is, the time came when we had to sit down! We had to devise a technique of gently pressing on the front, not too hard, and having the chair in exactly the right position, and then it worked. Sadly, more often, one of the hoops would spring out and make a show of itself, sticking out like a grotesque shelf, or worse, springing up to almost vertical and revealing all to the audience! We had to practice and practice to achieve some grace and success. I was particularly lucky as my dress was extremely full and heavy, but against that, I had to stand up to recite, in Victorian style, the 'Seven Ages of Man' speech, and the, horror of horrors, sit down again. On one evening, I returned to my chair and as I gingerly sat down I could tell that the hoop was wrong and if I sat down any further, it would spring, so there I crouched, hopefully only the pained expression on my face revealing the truth! It was nerve wracking!

We were depicting a family displaying their talents, their accomplishments. I had to recite and Beryl had to play the piano. This seemed a bit unfair as she remained seated throughout, and she was the one with the real crinoline! Joe Perkin arrived to pay suit to June and he sang a snatch of his song, and then the curtains opened to reveal the male voice choir who sang the whole of 'Pratty Flowers' with great enthusiasm.

If Beryl had been fortunate with her skirt, she was not so lucky with the hair. Ringlets were the order of the day, and Dad provided us with hair pieces from the shop, Grandad Strange having been involved with amateur theatricals in days gone by. I had lovely ringlets, just the right colour, but Beryl was fair and all that could be found for her were two blonde switches of hair which needed curling. Could her Mum put them in curl rags in time for the dress rehearsal? Oh yes, no problem there, said Beryl.

The dress rehearsal arrived and we all gathered excitedly into the corner allocated to us, organizing the wretched hoops, submitting to make up and the hair dresser pinning and combing and tweaking us into shape. Gradually we all became aware of Beryl who was sitting on a stool, unwinding the curl rags from the hair piece. The hair was slowly emerging, straight and lank, and Beryl was in tears. Total disaster loomed for her, what on earth could she do now? The hairdresser lady was a gem. She comforted Beryl, reassured everyone and explained that the hair had to be wound round the length of rag, and the rest of the strip of rag wound round the hair to hold it in curl, a procedure which Beryl's Mum had clearly forgotten. She actually did it for Beryl and fingers were crossed in the hope that it would work for the opening performance. Thankfully, it did. All was well, and honour restored

We all looked wonderful (apart from the odd mishap as I have explained) and all in all, it went extremely well. For the finale, the massed choirs were to sing the Hallelujah Chorus from the Messiah, accompanied by the band, and then all the cast were to assemble with them on stage for the final curtain. As space was so limited, our hoops had to be removed - no room for them in the squash We climbed the narrow steps up on to the stage, clutching our now very long skirts. The whole event was tremendous; tension, laughter, frantic activity both on stage and behind the scenes; a triumphant success.

I have many happy memories of the Dramatic Society, and especially of Auntie Elsie who was our main contact and friend there. She it was who included us in all the activities, and encouraged me, even to helping to find material for an audition with the BBC, for Northern Children's Hour, and rehearsing me for it.

I loved to go and spend the day with her in the holidays. She had a lovely grey tabby cat called, improbably, Tuesday. His mother had turned up at a friend's house one Monday morning, thus giving herself a name, and promptly gave birth to four kittens, Tuesday, Wednesday, Thursday and Friday. I thought this really good.

Visiting the toilet was always interesting at Auntie Elsie's. It was outdoors, down the garden, and shared by Auntie Len, Elsie's sister and her husband. It was a small stone building, with a pitched roof, almost hidden by the trees and bushes, and having a window with four panes, two of which were 'bull's eyes'; inside, along one wall was a wooden bench with three lids covering three holes of varying size! We were blessed with a flush toilet at Ivy Cottage so an earth privy was a bit of a novelty, quite draughty in the summer; freezing cold in the Winter. No electric light, of course, so after dark you had to take a torch, but three holes? I had heard of the Romans and their social attitude to bathing and wondered if this, in fact, was a Roman lavatory?

Auntie Elsie cooked on a gas ring, and in the side oven of her range. I have seen her mix a cake (with her hands, no wooden spoon) and open the oven door, put in a hand to check the temperature and declare it to be right, and sure enough, it was, the cake would be cooked to perfection. Such skill! When she did eventually have a gas oven, she loved its predictability, but always felt the cakes baked in the old side oven tasted better.

Then there was the shameful episode of the book. Both Auntie Elsie and Uncle George were very well read and had lots of books, many of which I borrowed. And one day I was allowed to borrow a copy of Hans Anderson's Fairy Stories, with strict instructions that as it was rather special I must be sure to take good care of it. I did, I enjoyed it immensely, some of the stories I could hardly read for my tears; 'The Little Mermaid' and 'The Match Girl' in particular, and in the holidays I took it with me to return it, when I visited for the day. When I arrived at Porch Cottage I was met by a girl called Dorothy, who was older than I, and she said Auntie Elsie would be back at lunchtime and we were to amuse ourselves until then. It was a fine day, so we set off through the garden and down to the river where we played around for a while, me still clutching the precious book. It was a hindrance, why hadn't I left it in the porch or on the steps? I shall never understand. When Dorothy said to leave it under the wall and pick it up later, I did so, but, it was forgotten and when I finally recalled it, I was too embarrassed to admit it was down near the river and I needed to fetch it. I went home and the book stayed where it was, and for some weeks I lay awake at night, wondering how I could secretly retrieve it. Misery hung around me, and guilty conscience, until eventually, I confessed to Mam in floods of shamed tears. The book was rescued and returned, but as could only be expected after it had suffered so much from the weather it was warped and 'skellered'. I felt so bad, so ashamed of myself, but Auntie Elsie, bless her, although hurt and upset, did not punish me. It was enough, she said, to see that my conscience had prevailed in the end. What a lovely lady she was. I remember my pain to this day, and she never held it against me. She and Uncle George gave me my first poetry book for my twelfth birthday. It was Palgrave's Golden Treasury and I have it still and have enjoyed it all through the years. Many years later, she recorded a tape cassette, in Yorkshire dialect, of anecdotes and local stories, in aid of the Macmillan Cancer Fund, called 'The Way We Were'; it is a treasure. She was such a talented lady and brought pleasure to so many people.

I must have started my Elocution lessons with Miss Hurst when I was about ten and I continued to enjoy them. Ella was a patient teacher and I have the feeling that I was her only private pupil. She worked for Madame Mitchell in Huddersfield on Saturdays. Madame Mitchell was the speech and drama teacher, whose pupils were often heard on the radio, but Huddersfield was a long way to go and her fees together with the bus fare were beyond Mam's purse. So, Ella it was and very well she taught me. During the day she worked as a mender in the mill as there was no way she could support herself by teaching Elocution. She was a lovely lady and she entered me for my first exams with the London College of Music. These were usually held in Huddersfield and Mam would take me to the rather fusty rooms in the top of office buildings, very gloomy, with brown paint on the walls and brown lino on the floors. One room in particular I recall, turned out to be a huge dance studio, complete with enormous mirrors and practice bar. When I walked in, clutching my copies, it felt as if I had to walk a mile to reach the examiner, seated at his table at the far end of the room. Although I probably had to present two poems, I can only remember one on that occasion. It was 'Nod' by Walter de la Mare, which I still love. I had a good mark and passed with flying colours, and had my name in the Holmfirth Express, the first of several such successes.

Probably the last exam I took with Ella was for the Poetry Lover's Fellowship, and it was in public; parents, teachers and other candidates made up the audience. I was very nervous. I had to say Coleridge's 'Kubla Khan', and I felt I had done rather well with that very difficult piece, and in fact, I was awarded a very good mark, but I was severely criticized for making a glottal stop on the phrase 'caves of ice'. I was very upset; the pain still lingers!

Holmfirth boasted its Competitive Musical Festival with classes for Verse Speaking, which I entered. The first poem I ever spoke there was 'Summer Voices' by Katherine Tynan, the first line of which starts 'Cuckoo and the corncrake...' I was well rehearsed and I marched on to the stage and stood on the piece of paper which had been thoughtfully pasted to the floor in the right position, but, nerves got the better of me and I started with the first line, 'Cuckoo...' and then stopped, realizing I had missed the title! What a humiliation for cocky Christine, and what a word to announce so clearly and confidently. I was the real cuckoo!

When I reached the age of fourteen or fifteen, Ella went to Mam to say she had taken me as far as she could, and suggested I might go to Jean Henderson in Huddersfield, but 'O' Levels were looming. I was at school in Penistone, and it was simply impossible for a while for me to continue. I did eventually re-commence lessons, with Mrs Henderson, and she it was who taught me up to and beyond London Academy Gold Medal.

I still remember her sitting room, with the embroidered fire screen on the rather gloomy tiled fireplace. We discussed which examining board I should go for. Should it be London Academy, Guildhall or RADA? The latter two were grade exams at my level, and you had to wait several weeks for the result, whereas with LAMDA, it was a Bronze Medal, and you had the result straight away. So, LAMDA it was, and it has stood me in good stead throughout my career. I was so proud of my medal, which duly arrived in the post, in a small box with the name of the medal-maker on it. My name and subject (still 'Elocution' at that time) were engraved on it. I was so thrilled, and so were Mam and Dad. Within the year I did Silver Medal and some two years later, Gold, when the term Elocution finally disappeared, and Speech became the subject's title.

It was to be many years before I used my knowledge and achievements, and made a successful career of teaching Speech, but throughout my life, those lessons with Ella Hirst and Jean Henderson were the source of tremendous joy which has grown and developed over the years. I wish I could tell them, but Ella moved to America; I married and had a family and moved away from Huddersfield, and I never saw Mrs Henderson again. I regret not looking her up on our occasional visits to Yorkshire. She worked so hard with me and her influence on me was incalculable. It would be so good to tell her about my girls, and how lovely they were, the work we did together, the exams passed, and the medals won.

CHAPTER TWELVE

Moving on ~ Penistone Grammar School

1949 was, I believe, the first time Holmfirth children had been allocated places at Penistone Grammar School in such numbers. Penistone was some distance away, with no direct bus route, and so a special school bus was started. Beryl and I were the only two pupils from National School; an older girl, Sheila, was already attending there and we were introduced to her, and she promised to keep an eye on us. Goodness knows how she made the journey before our Special Bus.

That first day was full of excitement, and with my new leather satchel on my shoulder (containing my shoe bag and plimsolls) and wearing my new black blazer with red braid around it, my navy gymslip with the dark red

Figure 12.1
Christine, wearing the all-important school blazer

185

girdle, and my black and red tie, I felt just like the girls in the books I had read, except they were invariably at boarding school! We were inordinately proud of the fact that our school was the third oldest in the land, having been founded in 1392, one hundred years before Columbus sailed the ocean blue and discovered America! It was not a historic building however. It was very conventional, and had the same smell of polish and milk and chalk dust that we were familiar with.

I was placed in the lowest class of all, Form 2 Remove. This was in a separate building at the lower end of the drive, and I duly found my way there with Beryl and everyone else. Having arrived in the classroom I realised to my horror that my new satchel was still reposing on one of the window sills along the main corridor, so, I had to explain my predicament and was sent to fetch it, 'and no messing about!'

'I walked the whole length of the corridor, which was still full of people, and I couldn't find the right window sill. Where could it be? Panic began to set in, until I realised I was on the wrong side of the corridor! In my anxiety I had completely lost my bearings. I have to confess that I am quite capable of doing the same foolish thing even now!

Why the lowest form should be the second form, I have no idea. The 'Remove' meant, in effect, C grade, with the possibility of being sent back to the secondary modern if one couldn't cope with the work, but I was blissfully unaware of this. Mr Hemingway was our form master; he was young, fair and handsome. The work interested me and I was in my element, and I loved moving around from room to room for different lessons, but mathematics, reared its head again, and Miss. Simm, a small lady with a square face, who always dressed in drab brown, terrified the life out of me. We were introduced to the mysteries of algebra and geometry as well as my old enemy arithmetic, and the mysteries mostly remained unsolved! However, somehow I must have coped, and plodded along at the bottom of the class. When I complained bitterly about it all making no sense, one day when we went to Auntie Jessie's house for tea, Derek, her son who was very clever and worked at the Huddersfield Building Society, said to me ,'Algebra is wonderful, Christine. With algebra you can even make one equal two; its magic!' He proceeded to do just that. I'm afraid his enthusiasm was lost on me. Frankly, if one could be made to equal two, the whole subject was absolute nonsense. How could one possibly be the same as two? Ridiculous!

Gym, I hated, and hockey I hated, but netball I hated even more. As there are only two positions in netball where you cannot shoot and score, and I was usually given one of them, I found the game totally boring. Hockey was marginally better, but I was invariably placed on the wing, and as the field sloped gently from one goal to the other, with a couple of small hills and a level patch, which was the cricket pitch, I spent a lot of time running and puffing hard, usually too far behind the rest of the forwards to be much use with Felix (our nickname for the games mistress, Miss Curry) shouting uselessly 'Where's the wing?' She was a very muscular lady, always to be seen in shorts, with a weather beaten face and very short hair. Actually, any outdoor exercise at Penistone was likely to make you weather-beaten; the school was on top of a bleak and windswept hill, and when it is cold anywhere else, it is very, very cold in Penistone.

I survived that first year, and in spite of my disastrous mathematics, I moved up, not to 3C but to 3B!

Accommodation at school was scarce, and in retrospect, the school was expanding rather more quickly than the space available. Certainly, for one term at least, our form room was the gym, which for me put a merciful end, for a while, to leaping over 'horses' and climbing ropes and wall bars. The new classrooms were made in what had once been part of the Headmaster's house, which meant that in our new form room we had an under-stairs cupboard which housed a gas meter. My friend Christine Thorp and I stayed in the cupboard all through French, one day, for a dare. It was a bit scary, in the dark, with the meter ticking away, but it seems we were not missed, and we were able to whisper the right answers through the keyhole to the boy whose desk was right beside the door. We were quite the centre of attention when we came out of our cupboard and felt very pleased with ourselves, until, at lunchtime, we met Miss. Senior, the French mistress, along the corridor. Suppose she realised we had been missing from her lesson? What would we say? All was well, she just passed us by.

There were always two or three Christines around, as it was a very popular name; my two best friends were Christine Roberts and Christine Thorp, both of whom lived on farms, and although we were seated alphabetically, we were still together as our surnames were, very helpfully, alphabetical.

It was a co-educational school in that boys and girls were in the same form, boys on one side of the classroom, and girls on the other. At dinner time, girls ate first in the canteen while the boys played, then we played while the boys ate. The boys had a separate playground, and, basically, never the twain could meet! Girls were addressed by their Christian names, boys were addressed by their surnames. Uniform was worn all the time although caps for the boys were very much on the way out. We girls wore berets, with the school badge. Many of the teachers wore gowns, especially the more senior of them. School began at nine o'clock and finished at a quarter to four, except for the Holmfirth contingent in the winter. As we had such a long journey across almost uninhabited countryside, there was always the danger of the road being impassable in the snow and ice. We would anxiously watch for the first snowflakes, or thick fog, and look forward to an early release from our labours. On several occasions, Mr Bowman the headmaster would come into our class, with his gown billowing, to say that the Holmfirth children should get their things together as the bus would be arriving early. Everyone was very envious!

Medical care was fairly basic. There was a sick bed in a cubicle on the top corridor, and very rarely, we would have a medical check-up when, it was rumoured, if you were wearing a bra, you would not be asked to remove it! We all campaigned hard for this precious piece of under-wear, but, predictably, it made no difference at all. A girl in my form was away for many months with TB, although the rest of us were never offered the now obligatory 'daisy prick'. One of the boys had a twin sister in another school, who caught polio. In fact, there was a serious polio epi-demic and we were all given the new vaccine on a lump of sugar, the Salk vaccine which had preceded it having proved disastrous.

I enjoyed the lessons on the whole and had con-sistently good marks, being placed within the top ten or twelve of my form, on average. Physics was a pain to me, totally incomprehensible, and Chemistry was much the same when it came to formulae. We did experience a quite serious accident in the third form. We were all gathered round one of the big lab tables observing an experiment to make water from hydrogen and oxygen, using sulphuric acid. Or might it have been hydrochloric acid? I can't now remember. Something went dreadfully wrong and it exploded, showering everyone with acid and burning one or two people who were near the front. Of course, I was near the back, and so escaped with a few splashes to my gymslip, but one girl, Judy, had acid burns to her face as well. It caused a great furore, and everyone was upset, and before many weeks had passed most of us were finding small holes appearing in our clothes, Thankfully, no lasting harm was done and even Judy's face recovered almost completely, but it shocked and upset everyone and experiments were rare in the days that followed

I enjoyed the lessons; well, I mostly enjoyed the lessons, with the usual exceptions. I had a lovely group of friends; I had no objections to the homework, there being no distractions like TV; I enjoyed the books we were set and the poetry and plays that we studied and on the whole the teachers were enthusiastic and very competent. It was a good time, exactly what experience of school should be. In spite of what would now be considered very limited sports facilities, we played tennis and rounders in summer, hockey and netball in winter; the boys had football and cricket and cross country runs. We enjoyed the usual summer races, high jump, long jump, javelin and discus, and I came last in almost everything except discus and tennis. Some girls were very interested in the boys, of course; they travelled to and fro from school with them, went to dances with them, jived with them, but there seemed to be no one very interesting on our bus, and everyone lived a long way from each other, even in Holmfirth. Social life was limited, but we visited each other's homes and always had to stay overnight because it was such a long way. Happy times!

My great friend was Christine Roberts, who lived on a farm, Chapel Stile Farm, at a tiny village called Midhope, just outside the small town of Stocksbridge. I went often to stay with her for the weekend, sometimes coming home on the Sunday afternoon and sometimes staying until Monday morning. For the first few visits it rained and many were the jokes about not allowing me to come at harvest time.

I was made very welcome there, and took a lot of teasing about how I must be very spoilt as I was an 'only one', and how everyone in Holmfirth said 'th'oven door'! This latter completely baffled me! They seemed to feel that their speech was infinitely superior to ours and had very strange notions about how we spoke. It was certainly different; the boundary between the West Riding and South Yorkshire lying at some vague point between our homes, but it was equally as distinctive as the West Riding dialect, and undeniably Yorkshire.

Living conditions at Chapel Stile Farm were primitive, and I realised what a very comfortable existence I had at home. Christine was used to life with no electricity, no hot water, and no bathroom or inside toilet. In the kitchen there was a large wide shallow stone sink, with a single tap coming out of the wall; in the living room, a large range with a fire which never went out, and on this fire Mrs Roberts cooked all the meals for herself and her husband; eldest son, Frankie, who worked on the farm; Christine; younger brother Vincent; the toddler Geoffrey and their 'farmer man' Josh, the labourer. On one side of the fire was the oven and on the other side, the boiler. A shelf above held anything that needed to be kept warm, and very high up, beyond that, a mantelpiece with a fringed cloth. It was much like the range that Mam had had removed from Ivy Cottage several years before.

In the middle of the living room stood a large square table with a variety of old dining chairs, a wooden rocking chair for Mr Roberts, and an old easy chair around it. A ham hung from the ceiling, and over the table, hanging from another hook was a large oil lamp. One window looked out across the fields and another window overlooked the yard.

Figure 12.2
With best friend Christine
Roberts at school.

The yard always seemed to be muddy. The cowshed, milking-parlour and pig sty all gave on to the yard, one side of which included a five barred gate for access. Opposite the gate, the house wall and kitchen steps, and the outside toilet formed the other side. Almost in the centre of this area was a well, and a goose! The goose filled me with terror, it was menacing in the extreme, hissing and cackling, and making short runs at anyone who came near. It had chased little Geoffrey and pecked him quite viciously and I was sure that its next victim would be me. I dreaded going to the toilet at any time of day, shivering in the cold and reading the squares of newspaper which were provided there, but at night it was even worse. For one thing it was pitch dark, so we had to take a lamp, a Tilley lamp, which had to be pumped up or primed. This alarmed me as I fully expected the thing to explode at any moment. It gave a good light, however, and hissed quite comfortingly as Christine and I made our way around the yard to the toilet, but, what if we wakened the goose? That didn't bear thinking about and we tip-toed on our way very cautiously.

At bedtime, Christine would beg for us to be allowed to keep the lamp (not the Tilley lamp, but a perfectly civilized paraffin lamp) for a while, and then leave it on the landing outside the bedroom door. It gave a soft gentle light, casting our shadows on the steeply sloping ceiling of her room. One little window overlooked the yard, and the other looked out across the fields. We slept together in her large comfortable bed which boasted a flock mattress, and the first thing Christine did when we went up to bed was to dive at this mattress and make a little hollow in it, for her to snuggle into. I quickly learnt to do likewise, and we would lie in bed and chatter away to each other until her Mum would request the precious lamp, and one of us had to get out of bed and put it, as promised, on the landing

We were wakened each morning by the soft rhythmic hum of the milking machine and the occasional lowing of the cows, followed by the sound of the cows being taken out to the fields for the day.

Mrs Roberts often cooked us bacon and eggs for

breakfast, unheard of at home! She had a very large iron frying pan, and to me, an amazingly generous amount of fat. Oh, the privilege of living on a farm in time of rationing. After breakfast we went out for a walk, following the little streams across the fields and up on to the moors, poking about in the water, making dams and generally splashing about very happily. We had such freedom, such unalloyed pleasure! Sometimes we had to deliver a can of milk to her grandparents and the way took us across a cornfield. The corn was high, reaching well above our waists, and we picked our way very carefully. When the corn was almost ripe, Christine would pick the ears and eat the contents, but I preferred to eat the peas which had been planted among the crop. They were sweet and delicious. Sometimes there were vivid scarlet poppies, too. It was a different world for me. The countryside I was used to was mostly for a few cows ; we were too high up and near the moors for arable crops and the hills were too steep for ploughing. I had sometimes watched hay being made in the top field across the valley from Ivy Cottage, but that had been my closest contact with actual crops. I found it all very exciting and when I visited in the summer at haymaking time, we were allowed to climb up the elevator and jump from the top on to the partly built haystack. It was great fun, and by today's standards, very dangerous.

If I stayed there on Sunday, we all went to Sunday school in the tiny whitewashed church, which had perhaps eight pews, ten at most. We sat around the iron stove at the back and received beautiful stamps to stick in a little book to register our attendance. I thought they were lovely and wished we had them at our Sunday school.

In the evenings, homework had to be done, and

we went into the parlour where Christine's mother would have lit a fire, especially for us. It was warm and cosy in the lamplight, with the fire flickering in the grate, and we told each other stories, played pencil and paper games and exchanged confidences; a secret, happy time. Christine was learning to play the piano and sometimes we had a go together, she telling me how to play the scale, and how to play 'Chopsticks' with her.

These visits were happy interludes and on at least one occasion I arrived home on the Sunday afternoon and felt very keenly the lack of brothers and sisters, to Mam's distress. Christine's life was so different to mine, so poor in many ways, especially the lack of comfort, but so rich in others; in the lively repartee and teasing and games with her brothers. Mr Roberts acquired a car on one occasion, (who did I know who had a car?) an ancient Wolseley, and they took me as far as the Flouch Inn road junction to catch the bus home. It was pouring with rain and the car leaked dreadfully. It was full of bits of straw and smelled of cows and pigs, and we sat on the old leather seat at the back in our raincoats and rain hoods. At school, Christine was able to announce airily that their car was a Wolseley, and they had given me a lift to the bus, a journey of some ten miles I suppose and I could bask in the reflected glory of having a car-owning friend.

It was our ambition to have a midnight feast, but our first attempt was not all that successful or enjoyable. We called at the village shop on our way home, but all we could buy was half a pound of arrowroot biscuits. That evening, we had cocoa before going to bed, a drink which I did not like very much. The biscuits were safely hidden under the bed and we managed to stay awake until we heard her parents climb the creaking stairs and close their bedroom door. We waited a while longer and then, out came the biscuits and we sat up in bed in the dim light of the moon and ate the lot. What more boring biscuit can you find than an arrowroot biscuit? In the morning, after the cocoa and the 'feast', I was sick, very sick, everywhere.

We had a more successful Midnight Feast when Christine came to stay with me, our village shop being somewhat larger than the one in Midhope. We bought sweets, and a few biscuits, crisps and lemonade powder (sherbert, or as we called it kay-lie). We hid it all in our satchels and the pockets of our gymslips and somehow managed to sneak upstairs with it and hide it in Grandad's old tin trunk under the bed. On my bedroom wall hung a Kelly lamp, a small paraffin lamp mounted on an oval tin tray which could be either hung up or stood on a table, the base of the lamp being weighted so it could never fall over. With the lamp in mind, matches had also to be smuggled upstairs. I was sure there was oil in the lamp as occasionally, for fun, Mam and I would take it downstairs and sit in its gentle light and in the glow of the fire make toast and listen to the wireless.

When bedtime came, we lay awake, whispering and giggling together, getting sleepier and sleepier, then rousing ourselves to wakefulness once more. Then we had the idea of one of us sleeping for half an hour and the other one keeping awake, and then changing over. We both had watches, but it was so dark we couldn't see the time! At long last, the stairs door opened and Mam and Dad came up to bed, and for a few minutes the landing light lit our room, and then the floorboards creaked as first Mam and then Dad went to the bathroom, and then to their bedroom and all was darkness again. We waited for what seemed an eternity before we felt it safe to light our little lamp and start the feast. I went to the bathroom to fetch some water, in the blue bathroom beaker, to mix the lemonade, and we sat up in bed eating our crisps and biscuits. It was great fun, even if the bed did get rather prickly with crumbs! When all was eaten, I crept back to the bathroom with the beaker, across the cold lino, avoiding once again the creaking floorboard by the door.

In the morning Mam demanded to know what we had put on the bathroom beaker. It was still covered in dried lemonade powder! Of course she must have realised we were up to some-thing, but she made no further comment when we looked innocent and said we didn't know what it was. She was a good sport.

Our third Midnight Feast was a complete failure. We fell asleep and didn't wake until morning.

What is it about the middle of the night that is so magical? Not just the darkness, or the quiet, or the feeling that no one is awake but you. Maybe it is the moonlight with its silvery glow, the stars and their mysterious constellations. I find it wonderful, and one of the great blessings when my sons were babies was the four o'clock feed, when I would stand at the bedroom window and look out at the sky, and sometimes see the stars begin to fade. Many years ago now, I had a period when I was wakeful during the night, for no particular reason, and I would creep downstairs, make a cup of tea and a slice of jam and bread, and together with my beloved cat, Monty, I would watch the moonlight on the garden. On more than one occasion, we would sit on the garden seat in the darkness of a balmy summer night and listen to the tiny sounds around us.

When Christine visited me, we followed much the same activities as at her home , did homework, listened to the radio, played games, walked the hills and went to

Church, which was huge by Midhope standards, and on Monday morning caught the school bus together. Or, we usually caught the bus. On one Monday morning we decided we couldn't face Double Chemistry so we determined to miss the bus. We dawdled down the hill, and walked very slowly round the corner by the Shoulder of Mutton pub, and into Victoria Square. The bus had gone! In that first instant, we didn't know whether to laugh or cry. We really had been left behind! Now what? We had to hang about for nearly an hour waiting for the bus to Shepley, and in Shepley we had another long cold wait for the other bus to take us as far as school. We arrived at break time feeling very self-conscious. Everyone was outside and came up to us demanding to know what had happened; we had to go to the Senior Mistress, Mrs Gathercole's office to confess we had missed the bus. That was a bit of an ordeal, but we got away with it. It was a triumph, and we missed Double Chemistry! Sometime later, I really did miss the bus, and that was not quite so enjoyable with no one to talk to. Again, I had to see Mrs Gathercole, and this time, I was reprimanded quite severely.

Apart from missing Chemistry, why did we play truant? We both enjoyed school and were well-behaved pupils who worked hard. I can only think it was a need to break out of the routine, to do something daring, to have an adventure like in the books which we read so avidly

I visited Eileen once. She lived in Stocksbridge, a small town built on one side of a valley, with Fox's Steel Works on the other, with the noise of machinery and lights even in the night. We could hear the noises as we went to bed. Eileen did elocution like me, and also learned to play the piano. Unbelievably, in their small terrace house, two up and two down, no bathroom or inside toilet, they had

installed a grand piano in the front room! It was a mon-
strous thing and left very little room for other furniture.
How they got it in there, I cannot imagine, but it was a
source of great pride. I only went there once, just overnight.

I once went home with my other good friend Chris-

Figure 12.3
Christine R. Julia, Christine S.

tine Thorp. She, too lived on a farm, more isolated than
Midhope. The nearest village was putting on a production of 'Iolanthe', and it was this that occasioned the visit.
We had a long cold walk across the fields from the bus to
the old farmhouse. It was large, severe and cold.   Like

Christine Roberts, they had no electricity and no warmth of welcome either.

Her mother was very quiet and I think she was quite intimidated by her husband, a stern, unbending, rather grim figure. They showed me a photograph of two boys who, many years before, had been the only pupils at Penistone Grammar School! Somehow, they were related to the family, and somehow the school survived!

I had the distinct feeling that they felt disappointed in Christine. She was a girl and they really wanted a boy. I felt sad about that. Christine was a very clever girl, but was very plain and wore specs. She attracted ink, glue and paint like iron filings to a magnet, even occasionally, dinner, in the form of gravy or custard, was to be found on her gymslip; her blouse always seemed to need ironing and her tie was like a piece of string. I liked her, and I enjoyed her company. Together, we enjoyed 'Iolanthe', walking there and back, in the dark, across the fields, and then, up the steep stairs to bed, in the dark. The bedroom floor was bare boards. The bed was hard and cold. I lay awake, watching the stars fade and the dawn begin to lighten the sky. Then, up we got, quick breakfast, and once again that long walk to the main road and the bus stop.

Christine was clearly proud of her farm and her family heritage, and on the way to the bus that cold grey morning, she stopped suddenly, and bent and picked up a handful of soil, and declared, 'One day, all this will belong to me!' The way I felt at that moment, she was welcome to it. It had been an ordeal for me and in all my time at Penistone, was only repeated once, but we remained good friends for the rest of our school lives. I have often wondered what became of her.

My other good friend was Linda. She lived in Holmfirth and we sat together every day on the bus. Linda was a quiet, refined girl, clearly much better off financially than us, and rather higher up the social scale, but she was good fun, and we were able to visit each other from time to time. She lived in a lovely old detached house in the centre of Holmfirth, next door to the doctor. I was very impressed; they had a front stairs and a back stairs, a dining room and a drawing room, both with beautiful windows which were almost floor to ceiling, hung with elegant curtains, and lovely carpets everywhere. The kitchen was huge, with room to set up a table tennis table. Her father was something important at the local newspaper, the Holmfirth Express. Linda played the piano, too, but not a grand piano, even in her lovely spacious house! Everyone seemed to play the piano except me.

And always, there was Anita. Anita was my first friend when we moved to Ivy Cottage, her Mum and my Mum had been school friends and had grown up together in Underbank, and lived just across Kippax Row from us. Anita was two years older than me and rather took me under her wing. We spent many happy hours together in her garden or ours, and possibly 'Our Game' derived from this play. Anita was two years ahead of me and when I was nine, she left National School attending Holme Valley Grammar; inevitably our paths diverged somewhat, but she was always a confidante, always good to be with and frequently called upon for help with homework, especially the dreaded Maths!

As time went by, interests changed and new friends were made and I saw very little of Olwynne. Surprisingly, I saw very little of Margaret too, although she followed me to Penistone a year later and we still met up at Sunday School and church, but, she was, of course, in a different form and as I had made new friends, so did she.

CHAPTER THIRTEEN

Moving up and Moving on

So, school days at Penistone Grammar were, on the whole, happy days. I worked hard and although I was never going to set the world on fire, I did reasonably well, except, of course, in Maths and Gym.

Winters came and I shivered miserably on the hockey field; summers came and I endured what felt like hours of boredom fielding 'deep' for rounders. Amazingly, when tennis was added to our activities, I found I actually enjoyed it, and what was more, I was quite good! Christine and I won the form doubles tournament to the astonishment of everyone, especially Felix, the games mistress.

As I moved up the school the work became more demanding and more interesting, and we were taught by the senior members of staff, who very often wore their gowns and were quite intimidating, at least at first, until we got to know them. G.C.E. 'O' Levels were looming ever nearer, but amongst all the hard work we enjoyed a few special treats and privileges.

The annual Speech Day was held in Penistone Town Hall, and only the older pupils could attend. The building, I seem to recall, also served as cinema, dancehall and theatre, and was simply too small for all of us. It was with some pride that we attended the great event when we arrived in the Lower Fifth, but found it fairly boring. The following year had more interest, when our examination results were announced and I was actually awarded a prize!

The Christmas Party was a great treat and I acquired my first real party dress for the occasion. It was crimson taffeta, with a sun-ray pleated skirt and short sleeves, and a neatly collared, small horseshoe neckline, revealing absolutely nothing but a small area of chest which would show off a gold chain, but, just in case it should be thought to be too daring, a white silk gardenia was strategically placed in front! It was lovely and I felt very grown up and sophisticated when I wore it. We also had a class holiday - no time off from school as it was actually in school holiday time.

We went Youth Hostelling in the Derbyshire Dales.

Figure 13.1
Mam and Christine,
aged sixteen

A rucksack had to be obtained, and one was finally acquired from a contact in the Dramatic Society. Good, comfortable shoes were needed as we were planning to walk ten or twelve miles each day. As I had by this time abandoned sensible shoes in favour of a casual pretty slip-on style, even for school, this posed a bit of a problem. It was eventually solved by using the old black lace-up shoes which I wore for hockey! Not much specialized footwear in those days , far too expensive for a duffer at games like me. The whole trip was such good fun; we enjoyed every minute, even the day when we walked through beautiful Dove Dale in the pouring rain. Somehow, we three Christines had become separated from the main party, and each time we brought out our map, it became steadily soggier, but, we found our way to the Hostel, and were very pleased indeed with ourselves.

The final year passed all too quickly, revising, or 'swotting' as we called it, taking up much of my time. I remember pacing up and down between the benches of the greenhouse, memorizing events, dates, formulae, speaking it all aloud to try to impress it on my memory.

All too soon, June arrived, hot and sunny, and suddenly there was no more time for revision. The school hall was no longer used for Assembly. It was all set out for the exams. Everyone had to be very quiet, not to disturb the unfortunate candidates. It happened every year, but now it was our turn to sit in the widely spaced desks. We could take nothing in with us except the pen and pencils that we would need, and not in our usual pencil tin either, in case we were tempted to sneak a few aide memoirs in with us! We were allowed a tube of Rowntree's Clear Gums, and the sight and taste of those sweets can whisk me back in time in a trice.

When the exams were all finished and I was anxiously awaiting the results, it was decision time. What was I going to do? Go into the Lower Sixth and set about 'A' Levels perhaps, and then what? Mam had always considered, when I passed for the Grammar School that I would be a teacher, but I had no ambition in that direction at all. Whatever I did as a career, I was not going to be a teacher! How ironic it was, that in later years I became a teacher! I taught Speech, Poetry and Prose speaking and reading for performance, for more than twenty-five years, privately and in a small independent school; I tutored adults for the Playgroup Movement, in College, taught children in Sunday school and I worked with young children and Special Needs children in Playgroup and Nursery. I loved it! After all, Mother knew best!

At that time, I was adamant that library work attracted me, being a book lover. When enquiries were made, I was told that even if I had a BA, I would still have to start at the bottom and do the shelving, and take the Library Association exams as I worked. Short-sighted as I was, college didn't seem too attractive, so why couldn't I start work now? I applied to Huddersfield Public Library, proudly giving my 'O' Level results, and with passes in seven of my eight subjects (no surprise that I failed Mathematics) I was quite confident the job would be mine. Interestingly, we were given no grades at all. The General Certificate of Education was quite new, and you were awarded a Pass or a Fail. Grades and the anguish they caused came much later.

The Library in Huddersfield was an imposing building of lovely mellow local stone, in the Art Deco style. There were two large stone figures, and a flight of shallow stone steps the full width of the building, leading up to the main entrance. Inside it was very grand, marble floors and a lofty ceiling, and yet more steps, leading to the Reference Library, and up again to the Art Gallery at the top of the building. The Lending Library was on the ground floor and it was huge. No marble floors in here, too noisy. The floor here was of quiet, warm cork tiles, with under floor heating. The book shelves were of beautiful solid oak, light and modern. It was impressive, a veritable palace to me, and to this grand palace, I was requested to attend for an interview.

The Chief Librarian conducted the interview, supported by several of his staff, at a long table in a stately ante-room. I felt I was doing rather well, saying the right things and, hopefully, giving a good impression, until the subject of working hours was broached. Every week, there were two days when I would be required to work until 7.30 pm and also on alternate Saturdays I would have to work until 7.30 pm Other days I would finish work at 5.30. Alarm bells began to ring! I had been given a part in the next Dramatic Society production. It was to be 'Pink String and Sealing Wax' by Roland Pertwee, at the end of October. How was I to manage the rehearsals, not to mention the performances? So I told them my dilemma. There was silence. Then a whispered conferring, and at last, the Librarian announced that as I was already committed to the production, I would be allowed to adjust my hours on this one occasion, 'But,'he said, 'the next time you are invited to play Ophelia, Miss Strange, you must decline!' That looked like the end of my acting ambitions, at least for the time being. Then, for the remaining weeks of the school holiday, I heard nothing. So, back to school I went in the September, to a completely different regime, and was expected to reduce my subjects to three or four. There were so many difficult decisions and I felt I was floundering, then, one Friday afternoon in October, Mr Bowman the Headmaster came into my class. My mother had telephoned the school to say that a letter had arrived from the Library for me. She had opened it and discovered they required me to start work on the Monday as a Junior Assistant Librarian! So sudden, so little time to say goodbye to my friends, collect my things, say goodbye and thank you to the teachers I had known for five years. That teatime, in a whirl, I took the school bus home for the last time. It was unreal and I didn't know whether to be glad or sad! What had I done? My life was about to change forever.

So it was that on the following Monday morning, Dad and I set out for work together, on the same bus to Huddersfield. How did I feel? Excited, apprehensive, like it was happening to someone else, still unreal.

That first day was probably the most exhausting of my life up to that point. Never, since I was a small child learning my letters, had I recited my alphabet so many times! Everything, it seemed, had to be in alphabetical order. Until, that is, I was taken downstairs to the Main Stack Room. This was a cavernous, gloomy place, with tall metal book stacks which were filled with dusty leather-bound volumes.

On the floor was a large untidy heap of copies of Hansard which had to be sorted into date order, and put on the empty shelves allocated to them. Well, it was a challenge, and a change from the alphabet! They were floppy paper-backed books, and, try as I would, they refused to stand on the shelf where I put them, they slithered and slipped and fell on to the floor and generally tried my patience sorely, but I battled on with the seemingly endless task until I was rescued and taken to the staff room for lunch.

The afternoon brought a couple of hours shelving in the Lending Library, walking round the huge room carrying armful after armful of books to be inserted into the sequence , back to the alphabet again! Then I had to be initiated into the Dewey Classification System for non-fiction ,decimal numbers this time, and each time I returned to the counter, a full trolley of books awaited me. It felt never-ending, and when I was required to, 'dump' armfuls of popular fiction on the top shelves just opposite the counter, and they all crashed to the floor, I felt quite desperate and near to tears. I bent to pick them up – ably assisted by the eager borrowers who were waiting for their next week's reading! The senior assistant was a kindly soul and came over to help and reassure. 'Don't worry, Miss Strange, you are doing fine. Just relax, press the books together, swing your arm up to the shelf, and push the books on to it'

After tea, I helped on the counter, date stamping the books which people were borrowing, sorting the book cards into numerical order. I had been unlucky to have started work on a 'long day', and at seven-thirty I headed for the Holmfirth bus.

Standing at the bus stop that cold October evening, I was more tired than I had ever been in my life! What a day it had been, and when the bus arrived, I sat down thankfully. My arms ached, my back ached, my legs ached and my feet hurt. My mind was reeling. Hard to imagine that only three days ago I had been at school and had almost given up hope of being offered the job of Junior Librarian. Suddenly, my life had changed I was in the working world, treated like an adult, and I.

would be paid at the end of the month! I already had a couple of books in my bag. I could borrow as many as I liked on my Staff Ticket, a decided bonus. There would be no long school holidays, no free Saturdays, and I would certainly miss them. I missed the idea of being a student, one of the elite Sixth Formers, at a Grammar School I was proud of and had enjoyed, but truth to tell, I had not enjoyed the work in the Sixth Form. I was taking too many subjects, being quite unable to decide which to keep and which to drop, and I was glad to put it all behind me and take up my new career. Now I was on my way to a play rehearsal, for which I was late, may be the last performance for a long time, but youthful optimism felt that anything was possible in my new life.

In spite of the tiredness, it had been satisfying. The staff were friendly and helpful. Of course everything had to be in order or no one would ever be able to find anything! There were so many new possibilities, qualifications to attain, specialist departments to explore, the Music Library, the Children's Library, magazines and periodicals, and the lofty hush of the Reference Library, all waiting to challenge and interest me. Added to this, I rather enjoyed being addressed as Miss Strange. The library was to be my life for the next four years until I married Keith.

I had left the pleasant green garden of childhood, and closed the gate behind me.

END